A BEDSIDE READER

TALES OF GROWING UP

LIVING AND DYING

Fr Terry

*Best wishes for all you do
in the future. Many thanks!
God Bless you
Love
Carol & Tom
Phil 4:13*

Thomas J. Miranda

*Thomas Miranda
June* .5

First published by Dog Ear Publishing
4010 W. 86th Street, Ste H
Indianapolis, IN 46268
www.dogearpublishing.net

ISBN: 978-1-4575-1203-2

This book is printed on acid-free paper.

Printed in the United States of America

FOR CAROL, WHO LOVED ME SO MUCH

TABLE OF CONTENTS

INTRODUCTION..1

PART 1 TALES FROM GROWING UP 3
A PRETTY GIRL...4
1-2-4-3..6
OLE'S CAR...8
AGULIA'S MAIL BOX...10
BRAKES...12
BURN COO 14
CENTIPEDE 16
BILL WAS SICK 18
AMATEUR HOUR 20
A STREETCAR NAMED RALPH..22
BLACK BADGE IN THE FIFTH 24
CLUB METRO...26
COWBOY MATCHES 28
CRACKED SEED...30
DOUBLE ROPE WASN'T FIRST...32
DOUBLE ROPE'S INGENUITY...34
MIOSAKE 37
EDDIE'S TAXI RIDE...39
EXECUTIVE STAFF..41
FEATURED SPEAKER..43
FRED WRIGHT'S COMING..45
FREE CANDY...47
FRUIT COCKTAIL..49
GOODNIGHT!!...51
HAOLE GIRLS 53
HAU..55
ICE HOUSE 57
LIBERTY THEATER 59
MOTORCYCLE HILL CLIMB..61

MARY BROWN'S FATHER 63

MY TURN, MY TURN...65

PIE BOY 67

PINEENEES 69

SHOOT HIM!!SHOOT HIM!! 71

SS HUALALAI 73

KANAKAS EVERYWHERE 76

THEY FIRED WHO…?? 78

TEST DRIVE...80

TOOTHACHE 82

WORD PROBLEMS 84

PART II SOCIO-POLITICAL ISSUES...87

THE BOZONE LAYER...88

BUTTER AND ROLLS 90

COMDOMS...92

EINSTEIN'S EQUATION...93

FO 95

FREE THE HOSTAGES...97

OLD SETTLER'S DAY 99

φτα...100

SEAT BELTS 104

STRINGS...106

REMEMBERING PEARL HARBOR 108

A SIMPLE SOLUTION 111

SLUMBER 113

SUPPLY AND DEMAND...114

TELEGRAM 116

TIM TEBOW 118

PART III EDUCATION AND INDUSTRY TALES 121

ALLYLBENZENE...122

BEHAVIORAL MODIFICATION 124

CHRISTMAS PARTY 126

HOW BEEG?...128

I USED TO WORK IN CHICAGO 130

INTERVIEW AT GENERAL ELECTRIC...132

LIQUID LITE..134

LIVING HINGE..136

LOOK UNDER THE BED 138

NO HOPE 140

OXIDATION-REDUCTION.............................142

SCHWAN SONG..144

PHIL'S REMEDY 146

PLANT TOUR 148

QUANTITATIVE ANALYSIS 150

RADIO OR PHYSICAL CHEMISTRY?...............154

ROCKFORD VARNISH 156

TAKE 'EM ALL...158

TALL OIL 161

THE ANNOUNCEMENT.................................163

THE DATE 165

TRADEMARKS 167

WHERE'S BUMONT?.....................................169

WRONG TURN-RIGHT PATH 171

WORRY 174

GOOD IDEAS; BAD RESULTS 176

THE DESK TOP 180

THE TOILET SEAT AFFAIR.............................182

PART IV REFLECTIONS 185

FINDING A TREASURE..................................186

CAROL IS BACK 188

WHERE IS MY PET?......................................190

CONFIRMATION 192

DONNA'S HERE 194

EASTER SEASON...196

GUIDE...198

HUMBLE 201

ONE THIRTY NINE 203

THE STATUE...205

THE PERFECT PARTNER.................................207

FAMOUS UNKNOWNS...................................209

SUMMARY 211

PREFACE

This book contains a collection of short essays from growing up in Hawaii, moving to California and his experiences during his high school years. After High school and college he found a real Treasure in and life companion sharing a 68 year love affair; love for nature and gardening, teaching music and basking in the Love of God who gave us so much

The character Grandpa Bigdog, GBD, was coined by my grandson Nick who was overwhelmed by the size of Eddie our large German Shepherd mix dog.

Topics covered are growing up tales in Hawaii and California, college days and working my way up the Darwinian ladder, political stories and tales gleaned from industrial and teaching experiences.

Hopefully the reader can glean a smile or living experience from the stories in this book and hopefully we can survive as the great nation we once were.

INTRODUCTION

I t was 2008 and America was caught up in an election year campaign featuring an Establishment Republican slate against a newcomer who was little known and from Chicago or from wherever. The Republican Party, the more conservative branch of the Democratic Party, had demonstrated another successful failure in the campaign earlier featuring Senator Bob (yawn) Dole were on track to produce another successful failure and losing the election!

It appears that Establishment Republicans had lost the road map to success that Ronald Reagan had drawn and have been wandering in the wilderness ever since.

The election of 2008 led to a number of land mark events not seen in America since this great nation was founded under brilliant God fearing men. The 2008 election was the triumph of the Insiders who had drafted the demise of America during their famous secret meeting at Jekyl Island in 1910 that gave us the Federal Reserve (which is not Federal and has no Reserves), the income tax and perpetual war, drained our treasury and destroyed the moral fiber of this once great nation.

With the election of Barack Hussein Obama, America changed course. Our Constitution is now reckoned as a piece of paper and the King now reigns by edict without the benefit of congressional oversight. Meanwhile, our Judiciary has become a sham and our fiscal sanity has gone amuck. We continually plunge deeper into debt with no hope for any common sense solutions. We are akin to the passengers on the Titanic, more interested in rearranging the deck chairs than fixing the gash in the hull!

America has gone from worshiping God to idol worship. The recent deaths of celebrities Michael Jackson, Whitney Houston and Anna Nichole

1

Smith received 24/7 coverage as though these drug addicted stars were worthy of this type of acclaim.

Volumes have been written concerning the decline and fall of our great country to no avail as we continue along a path to destruction. In our early history our moral compass was seated in the pulpits of our churches that shouted morality and decency as a way to national survival, but today we are preached that tolerance and compromise with evil is the best way.

Indeed this is a sad and unfortunate end to a once great nation.

In spite of this there are still memories and events in a person's life that are useful to remind us that there are still good people in the world and with Faith we may yet be saved from our own stupidity.

So let us instead reflect on some real life stories that happen in our journey to our next life and see if we can survive the reign of King Obama. Tales in this book include living events that can be humorous, a teaching moment or a revelation like the departure of a loved one.

PART 1

TALES FROM GROWING UP

A PRETTY GIRL

When Grandpa Bigdog was at Campbell High School in California the area had mostly fruit orchards and fruit processing plants. If one drove up to Blossom Hill Road in the spring he would witness a symphony of color as the different fruit blossomed. There were almonds that bloomed first, then cherries, then peaches, pears, prunes and apricots. The ripened fruit would be dried in dehydrators or out in the sun or canned.

In Campbell the Drew Cannery was a major force in canning apricots, pears, peaches and fruit cocktail. School would be out in June when Drew began to can apricots. In 1943 the apricots would be the first product. To process apricots there was a large elevated platform where many women and young girls would pit the apricots. From there a conveyer carried the apricot halves to a number of aisles where other women sorted the apricots and loaded them into cans. The pits and unusable apricots were disposed by the pie boys, which was my first job at Drews. The pits went to one conveyer, while the unsuited for canning cots went to make pie apricots for bakeries.

Behind this big operation were the fillers that filled the cans with sugar syrup and sealed the cans, then sent them to the steam cookers, then finally to the storage area to be labeled. Some of my friends who worked there included Mac Martin, Ray Flagg, Larry Hartley, Roy Zimmer, Bob Hall, Kent Clark, Jerry Finch and the hero of the story; Roy Prestogiaccomo who unfortunately was an ordained slob. Other than Ray and me the rest of these boys worked in the back of the cannery except for special times when they migrated to the pie aisles. During the course of the shift, the ladies took breaks and all had to parade past the packaging aisles where Ray and I worked and when this occurred the hound dogs were sure to gather there.

One of the prettiest girls was Marge Carmen. She and her sister Marie lived off Bascome Avenue where their father ran a nursery. Marge would walk slowly down the aisle while removing her rubber gloves and she was a sight to behold. After Marge left the hound dogs disappeared back to their stations until the next scheduled break remarking about her beauty and class.

One of the noble laureates, Roy Prestogiaccomo, would come over to Ray and I and tell us how much he liked Marge. This happened regularly, so Ray and I decided to help this Love bird move up the romantic ladder. Ray suggested to Roy that Marge was interested in him and that really started Roy's clock running. So, one day Ray and I wrote a note to Roy, signing Marge's name and suggesting that Marge would like to meet him tomorrow night in front of the Campbell Theater at 7:30 pm. So the next evening Ray and I went over to Clark's Drugstore to watch the romance bloom.

About 7:20 here came Roy all dressed up with a yellow jacket and green pants. We spent about 45 minutes watching poor Roy pacing up and down the sidewalk, but soon gave up and went home. The next day Roy told us of his long wait but Marge did not show up. So we gave him a number of scenarios of what might have happened.

At any rate Marge Carmen was indeed the prettiest girl at the cannery.

1-2-4-3

When Grandpa Bigdog lived in Campbell, California, he bought a 1927 Model T from Mervin Nelson for the huge sum of $5.00. This was a black coupe and it had no muffler, meaning that it could be heard around the whole town of Campbell.

Now this car did not run every day, so when I was lucky enough to start it, I would drive around town and pick up Mac Martin or Ray Flagg and cruise around making a lot of noise and having fun. This car was fun to drive and must have had a lot of history to it.

Soon GBD noted that other friends began to buy Model T's and drive them around town. Rex Jeffers bought a model T from Manuel (Pickinene) Miranda, our cousin, who owned an orchard on East Campbell Avenue.

One day Rex challenged GBD to a race. So we took off down Foote Street and up Hawthorne back to Campbell Avenue then back to Foote Street. Rex won the race easily. But, GBD noticed that one of the spark plug wires had come off his car. So GBD replaced the wire and challenged Rex to another race. This time GBD won easily and Rex decided that he had to make some repairs to his car.

GBD noticed a knock in the engine and decided to take the engine apart. There were quite a few bolts around the bottom pan of the engine, but eventually GBD got the pan off so he could see the connecting rods. Well two of the connecting rods were held on by only one bolt, the other having come off. No wonder the engine was knocking and it is a wonder that GBD did not throw a rod through the block. So after finding the necessary bolts and replacing the pan, GBD started up the engine. Well, you cannot imagine how much more power the engine had with all cylinders now properly connected to the crankshaft.

GBD's good friend Ray Flagg also bought a Model T, but it was not in running condition. So GBD went over to Ray's house on Apricot Avenue to help Ray get his car running. Well Ray had disconnected the ignition coils and the ignition wires. So we set out to fix the engine. Well, the Model T has four electrical coils, which produce 25,000 volts of electricity to fire the spark plugs. The wires from the coils go the distributor to fire a sparkplug when the piston reaches the top of the compression stroke.

So here is the mess Ray and I had. We were like the 'blind leading the blind' since we did not know the firing order of each cylinder. So GBD came up with an idea. He removed all of the spark plugs and had Ray crank the engine, while GBD put his finger over the sparkplug hole to see which cylinder had compression. When we got compression on the first cylinder we then connected the sparkplug wire to the first coil.

Now, what is the next step?

Well, GBD then figured that the firing order would be 1-4-2-3 so we attached the wires accordingly and began to crank the engine. To start a Model T one had to have the brake all the way on to push the transmission into neutral, then pull on the choke and hope for the best. Cranking a Model T is not much fun, and you had to be aware of backfire where the crank would snap backward and break a wrist.

When we got set we started cranking and the engine fired, sputtered and stalled. We were encouraged with this and cranked till we were exhausted. After awhile we abandoned this approach and tried other combinations. Each time we got some firing, but the engine never ran. We continued on this mission for a number of evenings with no avail.

One day a friend of Ray who was an auto mechanic came by and told us that we had the wrong combination. The correct combination was 1-2-4-3. We reconnected the wires in this configuration and lo and behold the car started and ran. Ray and I were delighted and soon Ray was riding around Campbell in his own Model T.

Later on Ray graduated to a Ford Phaeton sedan convertible and he used to ride around with Walt Trask and Nancy Alan and Sharon Wright. One day we were taking Sharon home and got a flat tire right in front of Sharon's home. So Ray and I struggled to fix the flat while Sharon sat on the running board waiting for us to finish the job, then we rode off down Bascombe Avenue up Hamilton then back to Apricot Street.

OLE'S CAR

Uncle Wally had an old Model T sedan and he used to drive around Kailua with this car. Some of the kids used to like to jump onto the running board and hang onto the car. So to prevent this Uncle Wally wired a Ford ignition coil to the car. The Ford coil could generate 25,000 volts of electricity and give you quite a jolt. Uncle Wally had a switch on the dash board to activate the coil so if someone would lean on the car he could turn on the switch and give them a surprise.

When Grandpa Bigdog was going to college, he worked as a movie projectionist at the Sunnyvale Theater in California. The doorman who took tickets bought a new Plymouth car and was very proud of his car. He parked it across the street from the theater where he could watch it. Across the street was a pool hall and the Nobel Laureates who frequented the pool hall would lean up against his car, making Ole very unhappy and he mentioned this to Grandpa Bigdog who suggested a fix for his problem.

GBD remembered what Uncle Wally had done to his model T and he had a Ford coil. So he told Ole that if he came by tomorrow GBD would wire his car with a Ford coil and put a switch on the dash. [The only problem was that GBD did not know how to wire the coil as Uncle Wally did.]

So next day Ole and a friend show up at GBD's house and he put a switch on the dash board and taped the Ford coil to the steering column. To get the biggest spark, GBD had to adjust the coil and you could hear….dee,dee,dee as the coil vibrated. So GBD told Ole to turn on the switch so he could adjust the coil.

So GBD began adjusting the coil, ...dee,dee,dee

....dee,dee,dee and the car began to shake violently as Grandpa Bigdog tried to adjust the coil. Finally GBD looked up and there was Ole and Jackie bouncing all over the car trying to turn off the switch. Finally GBD disconnected the coil and the two victims jumped out of the car, white as sheets.

You see GBD had reversed the wires and gave them the shock instead.

AGULIA'S MAIL BOX

Growing up in Honolulu was an interesting time for Grandpa Bigdog. There were certain holidays that we kids really looked forward to. The serious holidays were Christmas, Easter and Memorial Day, while New Year's and Halloween were more fun days.

Halloween was especially fun and we used to prepare for that event weeks in advance. One of the things we used to do was to make stink bombs. The idea was to create a foul smelling mixture that we could throw on someone, who in turn had made his own stink bomb to get even.

Uncle Paul and GBD used to try to develop the foulest odors we could dream up. We started with bluing, which was used in washing clothes in those days. Bluing is a dye made from Prussian blue an iron compound and when used on clothes, tends to hide the yellow that might develop in the washing process. Today with modern detergents, we don't use bluing anymore.

The other event we always looked forward to was to develop bombs to see who could blow up a mailbox. Most mailboxes were small stamped steel units that hung on the gate and we used to get a charge from putting a large firecracker into the mailbox and lighting the firecracker, then running like crazy. Most of the time the mailboxes would be blown off the gate or if we could come up with a stronger bomb, blow the lid right off the box.

Enter Agulia! Agulia was a Portuguese lady who lived on Auwaiolimu Street who did not like us kids too much....and for good reason. I don't know what her real name was, but we all called her Agulia, which in Portuguese means needle. Well Agulia had a welded steel mailbox mounted into a concrete gatepost and that was the problem.

Every Halloween the kids tried to blow her mailbox up with out success. Some would collect old firecrackers and extract the gunpowder, then make their own bombs all for the purpose of getting Agulia's mailbox and without success.

Enter Uncle Wally!

Uncle Wally decided that this was his big challenge, so he made a special firecracker (I won't tell you how he did it) and he thought that this would work. So on Halloween night we went through all our usual routines, making noise, throwing stink bombs, and stealing mangos from Mrs. Ornellas tree then finally settling down to the serious business of the night…Agulia's mailbox.

So each challenger approached the mailbox, dropped his lit bomb into the box and ran for cover. This was followed by a big bang, but the mailbox survived each time. No one could come close to budging this steel structure until Uncle Wally came up with his specialty. All the kids were laughing and taunting him that he too would fail. Uncle Wally ran up to the mailbox, lit the fuse, dropped the charge into the mailbox and ran for cover.

There was a huge bang and the clattering of steel and concrete as Agulia's mailbox went flying out of its concrete base and landed on the street twisted and torn.

Well, Uncle Wally became a local hero and all the kids marveled at his success in overcoming the powerhouse that was Agulia's mailbox.

BRAKES

How do you stop a skate car? Well we never gave much thought to that as Uncle Paul and I used to take chances pushing each other up and down the sidewalks on Lusitana Street in Honolulu. When we went down Kuakini Street that was steeper, we usually made it to the bottom of the hill and could use our feet to stop. But if we tried to ride our skate cars down Pouwaina Drive it was another story. Pouwaina Drive was smooth and all down hill until it merges into Lusitana Street. So once we got started down the drive there was no stopping so we devised a brake by pounding a stick into the frame of the car and dragging it on the pavement to stop.

Uncle Wally had come upon some ball bearings used on automobiles and these made great rear wheels for our skate cars. They were about 3 inches in diameter and turned so easily. The only drawback was that we had to take a 2x4 and spend hours rounding out the ends to fit the ball bearing race onto the axle. Uncle Paul used to spend hours sanding and cutting the wood so we could fit the race onto the wood. Then we pounded nails into the wood to expand the wood to hold the bearing in place. We also made the skate car larger so that both of us could ride.

We finally finished the new skate car and decided to go for a test ride. This always involved pushing each other up and down the sidewalk on Lusitana Street, then flying down Kuakini Street. On Kuakini Street we tried out the brake and it was able to stop the skate car.

We then decided to go for a real ride. We dragged the skate car up Holy Ghost hill to Pouwaina Drive then up to San Antonio Street. This gave us a long sloping ride all the way down to Lusitana Street and since we had brakes we could stop before we ran into an HRT bus.

So we piled onto the skate car and started down the road. What we did not expect was the speed we were achieving with the new ball bearing wheels. As we raced down the street Uncle Paul started to apply the brake but we didn't slow down very much. We were getting closer to the end of Pouwaina Drive where it merges into Lusitana Street so Uncle Paul really applied the brake and it came off in his hand. So here were racing down the street with no brakes and a possible accident.

At the last minute, Uncle Paul turned into Madeira Street to our left, which is the last street before the intersection. (This street is as steep as Holy Ghost Hill and one that the Police Department uses to test drivers who apply for a license.) Our skate car ground to a halt and we had to drag it back home to fix the brake. So the ball bearings gave us a lot of speed, but a beeeg scare!

BURN COO

During the depression (1929-1939) more than 25% of the workforce was out of work and many people suffered. In order to solve this problem, the New Deal designed by the Roosevelt Administration decided to create jobs through government largess. The result was that many programs were put into place, such as the Civilian Conservation Corps (CCC), the Work Projects Administration (WPA) and other such socialist handouts.

The CCC was instrumental in building trails, rest havens and roads in the National Forests and creating public works like fountains, parks, band shells. The WPA employed many people in projects like road building.

GBD's first exposure to the WPA was a project on Auwaiolimu Street where we lived in the early depression days. The WPA crews built curbing on the street from large blocks of stone. In order to split the stone they had to use rock chisels, hammers and sledge hammers. In addition to building the curb, they also built stone retaining walls along the street. Now since Awaiolimu Street is on the slopes of Punchbowl Crater, retaining walls were very necessary. They built these walls up past Mrs. Freitas and Sonny Ornellas homes up to the famous Chinese graveyard.

There were quite a number of men doing a lot of manual work (no bulldozers in those days) and the locals would come out to watch them during the day. In addition to Uncle Paul, Uncle Wally, Gilbert Dias, Guava and Ah-ba-gee, there were a bunch of old Portagees who were retired and they were always talking about the days when they worked in the cane fields or the pineapple cannery.

One particular guy who had a high vapor pressure was Mr. Bettencourt, a large man with a big potbelly who wore thick suspenders to hold up his pants. In addition to being quite loud, he also offered a lot of free advice to the workmen, who did not always appreciate him sticking his nose into their business.

After finishing the work on Awaiolimu Street, they moved up to Puowaina Drive and set up shop just above the Chinese Cemetery. A blacksmith shop was set up there to make chisels, sledge hammers and other tools needed to break the rock. The blacksmith had a big forge and we used to like to crank the blower to make the fire hot. Well, guess who showed up?

Mr. Bettencourt and his team of experts to give the blacksmith a hard time i.e. council..

One day Mr. Bettencourt was holding court and getting under the blacksmith's collar. The blacksmith was heating a large sledge hammer in the forge that was now red hot! About that time, Mr. Bettencourt saw a piece of string on the ground and bent over to pick it up.

This was the blacksmith's chance to get even. He took a large pair of tongs and grabbed the red hot sledgehammer head and brought it very close to this large bent over Portagee's coo. You should have heard the yelling as Burn Coo was dancing around trying to cool off. That day he acquired a new nickname and Uncle Paul and I learned a few new words (that couldn't be used in church.)

CENTIPEDE

Have you ever seen a centipede? A centipede is an arthropod with many legs. Most of the centipedes we have in Indiana are about an inch long and relatively harmless. But the centipedes in Hawaii are huge. They are seven to eight inches long and have a terrible sting. They usually hide out under boards or rocks or in dark places like shoes or boots. So we always shook our boots out before putting them on at Double Rope's dairy.

I can remember Auntie Annie's garage in the front yard of her home in Kailua. At the rear entrance there was a board lying on the ground and one day my cousin Walter and I walked into the garage and knocked over the board and there was huge centipede...a very ugly creature.

One of the worst experiences Grandpa Bigdog had with a centipede was when we lived on Auwaiolimu Street in Honolulu. One of our favorite night games was playing hide and seek. One night Uncle Paul, GBD, Pig, Uncle Wally, Sonny Ornelas some other kids were playing hide and seek and GBD climbed up a stonewall on Whiting Street next to a garage. As GBD put his hand on the top of the wall, he felt a terrible pain and yelled out. One of the kids had a flashlight and there was a large centipede crawling away.

GBD had put his hand right on the centipede and got stung. Well the aftermath was not good. GBD went home crying and Grandma Olivia put some Rawleigh's ointment on the sting. (Rawleigh's ointment was the all purpose medicine, for everything and that blue and gold can of ointment was forever embedded in our memory). Well the next day GBD spent a miserable day in bed with a fever until the effect the sting and the pain wore off. So you can see why we steered clear of these creatures.

Uncle Joe (Double Rope) had a dairy and to milk all his cows he had to hire some executive assistants, many of whom were real characters. Barriga was a guy with a big pot belly and it was a wonder how he could reach around to milk the cows. Another executive was a guy named Manuel. He was born with congenital laziness, first to dinner, last to work. He was the slowest moving creature GBD had ever seen. Double Rope used to get so angry with his slowness.

One day Double Rope decided to speed him up. So Double Rope found a big centipede and dropped it into Manuel's boot. Around milking time Manuel showed up, in slow motion, and began to put on his boot. Within a millisecond there was Manuel dancing around howling and yelling until he got his boot off. This had to be the fastest thing he had ever done in his life and Double Rope and the other around him had finally gotten some speed out of him, thanks to the awful centipede.

BILL WAS SICK

When one is growing up he may meet a lot of people on the way up. These include family members and friends and acquaintances in school. Some become lifelong friends while others are people who are just passing through and are never seen again or thought much about. On the other hand some of the people you would never think about become quite famous and you would not have imagined that would become important in later life.

Here are some examples.

When I was a student at Campbell Union High School in California there were some friends that I still remember to this day. Paul J. Meyer was a good student and accomplished at athletics. In fact, everything he did he did with the aim of perfection. Once his father bought an old junk car and took it apart completely laying all the parts on a tarp on the driveway. Then he told Paul that if he could assemble it, it was his. Well, assemble it he did and drove it off.

Another student was Bill Wilson better known as Billy Wilson who was an outstanding athlete. He excelled in all sports and was an end on the football team. He was one of the big stars when Campbell High won the division championship. Bill later attended San Jose State College and was later drafted by the San Francisco 49ers. There he became a great star and played with such champions as Y. A. Tittle, J. D. Smith and R. C. Owens, who was known as "Alley Oopp" because he would leap high into the air to catch passes from Tittle. It was said that when Billy Wilson went out for a pass he would catch the ball whenever it was near him.

One of Bill's pals was Roy Zimmer who lived on Milton Street just behind the Campbell High stadium. Roy and Bill played on the football team and it seemed that everywhere Bill was there was Roy. Roy was a real big time operator who after graduation ran a gas station on the corner of Winchester and Campbell Avenue.

The weather in Campbell was great. There was no rain from Memorial Day until early October. As a result the hills became golden in color as grasses on the hills and mountains dried out. When the rains came, the entire Santa Clara Valley was ringed with a beautiful carpet of green as the new grasses grew. Looking East from Campbell Avenue was the foothills and in the distance Mt. Hamilton where the Lick Observatory is located. Sometimes in the winter snow fell on Mt. Hamilton and it was a great treat to go there and play in the snow.

Well, one day it snowed and some of the students skipped school, including Bill Wilson and Roy Zimmer. There was nothing wrong with skipping school, but when you returned you had to face **Miss Nielsen.** She was an Assistant Principal and Student Councilor and a real tough lady who did not put up with much nonsense.

So when Bill and Roy came to school the next day, their first stop was Miss Nielsen's office.

"Bill, why were you not here yesterday?" she asked.

"Well, I was sick" said Bill.

Then she turned her eagle eye on Roy and asked him why he was not in school.

"Well, Bill was sick so I went over to his house to keep him company", was Roy's honest answer.

With that it looked like they were off the hook. Miss Neilsen showed some apparent sympathy for these stalwarts and asked a few more questions before dismissing the pair. But, just before they left, they noticed a folded copy of the San Jose Mercury News on her desk. She asked them if they had seen the morning paper, which they had not.

There on the front page was a large picture of Bill Wilson and Roy Zimmer playing in the snow on Mt. Hamilton.

Bill and Roy should have listened to Mark Twain who said, "**When in doubt, tell the truth, it will please your friends, amaze most people and confound your enemies**".

AMATEUR HOUR

Tonight on TV will be American Idol and millions will watch this program and cheer for their top amateur. This program reminds me of the Amateur Hour on radio when I was growing up in Honolulu. This was a very popular program and people who were rich enough to own a radio could listen to this program and cheer for their heroes.

We lived on Awaiolimu Street about four doors up the street from Mrs. Cosme who owned a radio. So on every Wednesday evening at 7 pm Mother, Lorraine, Paul, Eve, Wally and Grandpa Bigdog would be at Mrs. Cosme's house to listen to the program.

There were some who eventually became famous like Hilo Hattie who used to sing "When Hilo Hattie does the Hilo Hop there's not a bit of need for a traffic cop". That song became a favorite for many years and most people remember her for that song. Other famous singers were members of the Honolulu Rapid Transit company and they eventually had their own program with a theme song, "Down by the barn on Alapai Street, there's a bunch of jolly good boys you will meet, they work for HRT, they spend their time of day, down by the barn on Alapai Street".

There were other more unfortunate competitors who would be stopped by a loud gong if they were poor performers. Once in a while we would hear someone we knew in the neighborhood doing animal impersonations or playing a harmonica or singing.

The last contestant usually finished a few minutes before eight o'clock and we all stood up, thanked Mrs. Cosme then started for home which only took a few minutes. As we reached our front gate, we could hear the theme music blaring from Mrs. Fernandez house that was a few doors up from our house and higher on the slopes of Punchbowl. We always got a kick out of hearing the end of the Amateur Hour coming from her radio.

A few years later, our cousin Peter, Auntie Annie's son bought us a small table radio and we used to enjoy listening to Little Orphan Annie. But the scariest of shows were at night when they played "I Love a Mystery". The theme song was Sibelius' Waltz Trieste and it was really scary music for us. The other great shows were the Lone Ranger and The Shadow.

If I had my choice today, I would rather be listening to the Amateur Hour and those old shows rather than to American Idol.

A STREETCAR NAMED RALPH

Tennessee Williams wrote a play entitled "A Streetcar Named Desire" that played on Broadway then later made into a movie starring Marlon Brando. The event takes place in New Orleans and involved a woman coming by train to New Orleans and asking directions to get to her sister's home and was told to take a streetcar named Desire. I have been to New Orleans a number of times and have actually seen this old green streetcar.

Speaking of streetcars, I am reminded of a story I heard many years ago while I was a student at Campbell Union High School in California. We had a number of great teachers there and one of them was a basketball coach named Ralph Noddin. He was a short thin man who probably weighed no more than 125 pounds. He was also a great disciplinarian and the Physics Teacher. Anyone who really studied physics under Mr. Noddin would have no problem with physics later in college. He had a funny way of teaching that showed his discipline. During a test he would read a question only once and the students were given time to respond, then he would go on to the next question.

One day during one of his tests Phil Ling asked him to repeat the question and he refused. Phil proceeded to challenge Mr. Noddin but he would not back down. Soon this event turned to a real shouting match between the two, but Mr. Noddin held his ground. That was quite disruptive for the class.

In our physics class Mr. Noddin had a large armature of a direct current electric motor that he used to demonstrate electrical applications. One day I asked him where he got the armature and he told us that is was a rotor used in electric motors to drive a streetcar. He then went on to tell us a tale about his college days at the University of California in Berkeley.

It seems that the members of the football team befriended him and he became an important asset to them in carrying out selected pranks. There was a streetcar line that went from downtown Berkeley, past the Cal campus and ended at a city park. So the football players and Ralph Noddin would board the streetcar as it came past the campus and rode to the end of the line near the end of the evening.

When the streetcar reached the end of the line on its last run of the night, the motorman would leave the streetcar with his girlfriend and take a stroll through the park. This is where Ralph Noddin played a key role! He was the only one who knew how to drive a streetcar, so he would get out and switch the trolley line then move the controls to the front of the streetcar and they all joy rode into downtown Berkeley leaving a flustered motorman without his streetcar.

There is a school named after Ralph Noddin in San Jose, but I don't think they mentioned the streetcar.

BLACK BADGE IN THE FIFTH

When Grandpa Bigdog was in high school in Campbell, California he used to obtain summer work in Drew's Cannery. My first job was a 'pie boy' who served the ladies who were canning apricots and peaches. This was a night shift job and the ladies were quite bossy. After a season of this, GBD decided on a better career opportunity. The next season I got onto the maintenance crew as an electrician's helper. This job was more reliable because when the fruit season expired there was still a lot of work to do wiring motors, changing electrical units and other tasks.

Later on Drew's Cannery was acquired by Hunt's Foods. Some of the people I remember on the crew included Carl Venable and Lloyd Martin [Mac Martin's older brother]] and Vintro an old Portagee who would never use a level in building platforms. He always had a habit of borrowing my tools and never returning them.

Our shop was next to the boiler room and Lou Genaci, who was also the business agent for the union, ran the boilers. On the second floor of the cannery we had a motor storage room where we kept spare motors. It was also a good place to hide out and play cards when Fluffy, the Plant Superintendent [Joe Silva] was not looking.

One day a conveyer motor quit and I tried to restart it, but it was burnt out so I told Fluffy that I would have to replace the motor. This was important since the whole cannery was shut down while I replaced the motor. But the maintenance crew who had to dismantle the conveyer was nowhere to be found. So Fluffy and I ran up to the second floor where I had a spare motor and lo and behold, most of the crew was there playing cards. You should have seen the scramble like group of cockroaches when the lights go on.

One afternoon as I was in the shop I saw a man approach Carl Venable and hand him some money. I ask Carl what was going on and he said that that man was the bookie and he was paying him off for his winnings in the horse race. Carl showed me a racing form and told me that all I had to do was pick some horses and tell the bookie. So I chose two horses and gave him the names and forgot about it. A week later the bookie showed up looking for me and counted out fourteen dollars, took back two, then proceeded to count out $34 and took back two for his fee. I asked him why he was doing this and he told me that my horses had won in the race.

This turned out to be fun and I found myself actively reading the racing forms and placing bets with the bookie for the rest of the summer. I was doing pretty well until summer ended and it was time to return to school and my job and income was gone. As a final gesture I decided to bet on Black Badge a horse that I was following weekly. I told the bookie to place a bet in the fifth for Black Badge to win, and then waited nervously to get the results.

So Sunday morning after church I went over to Shadle's drug store to check the paper. Well Black Badge did not even show and I was now in debt to the bookie for $2 and no way to pay. Lucky for me I got a small check from the Campbell Theater where I was also a projectionist and was able to pay the debt.

This was a good object lesson and certainly cured my desire to bet on horse racing.

CLUB METRO

After graduating from San Jose State College, Grandpa Bigdog obtained a General Secondary Certificate so that I could teach in a California High School. One of the last functions before obtaining the certificate was to Student Teach in a high school, which in my case was Los Gatos High School. I taught two classes Chemistry and Advanced Algebra. I really enjoyed teaching chemistry and did very well, but I had some problems in the Algebra class since I took over the class when they were learning word problems. You know, A can run 3 times faster than B and C can only run half as fast as B. How fast can D run?

What made it worse was my adviser Dr. Herman Jameson who never liked me and always gave me a hard time. He made it a practice to drop in unexpectedly on my class and if I made a mistake he would call out from the back of the room that I was wrong. The resident teacher noticed the friction between Dr. Jameson and me and one Friday afternoon had a long talk with me to encourage me. He also mentioned that I should be very careful in my outside of school activities because it could hurt my teaching career; like being seen in a bar.

One of my good friends is Mac Martin. Mac played first trumpet in the school band and later learned the saxophone and the string bass. Mac played in Bill Smith's Orchestra with Doug Strong and Bill Harrison. They would play at Campbell High School dances or the Prom. After High School, Mac entered the army and served in the Army Band in Adak, Alaska. After his service Mac returned to San Jose State where he graduated. Mac also played in several orchestras some of which were bars like the Metro Club located on Alum Rock Park Road.

There were many Okie bars around San Jose where cowboy songs were the stock and trade of the musical entertainment. Other activities included fights, lots of noise over the band and the possibility of losing one's reputation.

Well, Mac got a job playing the string bass at the Metro Club and told me to drop by some evening. I hesitated for some time for two reasons. First I was student teaching and wanted to be careful of my reputation and secondly I worked as a projectionist at the Sunnyvale Theater and did not leave work till after 11:30 pm or later. Well Mac was a bit persistent so one evening after work I decided to go to the Metro Club, besides no one would know me there.

Luck was on my side as I drove from Sunnyvale to the Metro Club. As I approached the Club some drunk Oakie backed his car into an oncoming car and there was a big crash. This was my first bad omen. But I persisted and entered the club where the pandemonium was awful. I knew no one there and stood by the bar for a few minutes and decided it was time to go. As I started for the door, Mac spotted me and called me up to the safety of the stage where I stood by his string bass. After awhile some lady asked the leader of the band if he knew "AHM SENDING YOU A BIG BOQUET OF ROSES" to which he said "No". Foolish GBD replied that I knew the lyrics so I took the mike and started singing and the band picked up the beat but I sang to fast almost fouling up the tune. As I was half way thru the song in walked Lowell Gratton, his girl friend and another couple from Campbell High and they started laughing. I had been seen in a den of iniquity.

Lucky for me the word never leaked back to Dr. Jameson or Los Gatos High School.

COWBOY MATCHES

When we were kids growing up in Honolulu we did a lot of things to keep busy, some of which got us into trouble. For example, on Halloween night we would try to concoct stink bombs made from bluing, rotten eggs and vinegar or make explosives to blow up mailboxes.

Since we grew up during the depression, there was little money around and not too many people had jobs. As a result only the rich kids could go to movies or buy semoi. (Now rich meant that some kid had enough money (ten cents) to go to the movies). When we could go to th movies our favorite theater was the Roosevelt Theater and they showed a lot of Western movies with stars like Hopalong Cassidy, Tim Holt, Gene Autry, Ken Maynard and Tom Mix.

For those who couldn't go to the movies, we would try to corner one of the rich kids to tell us about the latest cowboy movie. We listened with great interest to detailed descriptions of the hero and what he did to round up the bad guys. We also were interested in the chuck wagon, cattle rustling and stampedes.

One of the interesting things about these movies was to watch the hero roll a cigarette from a bag of Bull Durham and reach into his pocket for a match and strike it against his boot to light his cigarette. These of course were strike anywhere matches which we named Cowboy Matches. We thought that this was really neat and a characteristic of movie cowboys.

Most of the matches we had were safety matches, which require scratching the match head on the side of the box to light the match. This worked well in Honolulu since we had natural gas for lighting our stove. But, in the country there was no natural gas, so I remember Auntie Annie using cowboy matches to light her kerosene stove.

Uncle Paul and I attended Cathedral School on Nuuanu Street with our good friends Eddie, Walter and Johnnie Medeiros. One day one of the kids brought a bunch of cowboy matches to school and during recess was showing them off. One of the tricks he did was to throw the match hard onto the sidewalk and the match would light.

Well after school Uncle Paul, Eddie, Walter, Johnnie, Willie Olivera and Stanley Machado and I were walking home and we all got some cowboy matches. Leaving school we headed up Nuuanu Street and turned onto Kuakini Street. Each of us tried to outdo each other in striking cowboy matches onto the sidewalk. Along the way was an empty lot with a lot of weeds in it.

When we got to Fort Street we heard people yelling "**FIRE**". As we looked back we saw the empty lot ablaze. There was a fire alarm on the corner of Fort Street across from the Poi Factory and one of us pulled the fire alarm and in a few minutes three fire trucks showed up and put out the fire. We were all wondering if we could get credit for turning in the alarm, but no one asked us so we went on home.

Twenty years later, I was thinking about that incident when I realized that it was we kids who had started the fire. Was I glad they did not ask us about that.

Remember, Don't Play with Matches, especially cowboy matches.

CRACKED SEED

W hen Grandpa Bigdog lived in Honolulu we used to crave Chinese candy. We lived on Boyd Lane that is a small lane running off Lusitana Street. Eddie and Walter Medeiros lived on Lusitana street. Across the lane from our home were four homes owned by Mr. Boyd. Two of his children were our playmates, Kekaa and Maddie.

One of our favorite Chinese candies was Cracked Seed. When and if we ever had enough money, that is a nickel, we would trudge up to Chun Ho Lee's Store and buy a package of Cracked Seed. This I believe was made from prunes and the seed was crushed and mixed with the prune fruit. VERY ONO!! The purchase involved a lot of thought, decision making and the torture of looking at all the big glass jars full of sweet, semi-sweet and sour (sawa) seed and red and white ginger and mango seed, footballs (preserved olives). Then came the problem of spending the fortune, five cents, and the difficulty of sharing the treasure. Because we usually had company to assist in the purchase and they were all eyes as the Cracked Seed was scooped into a small brown paper sack hoping that we might get more for our money.

Here is how we ate the cracked seed. We would squeeze the bottom of the sack and slowly force a piece of cracked seed up the sack and pass a piece to one of friends making sure only one piece escaped. The owner of the package (whoever had the nickel) was watched closely to make sure everyone got a fair share. We carefully nurtured the package until all the seed was consumed. Now came the tricky part; splitting the bag. For example Walter, Eddie and Uncle Paul and Grandpa Bigdog would participate in this critical step. GBD would tear the bag in half, and then tear the half in half. One piece went to Walter and one to Eddie. Then GBD would tear the bottom piece in half and give Uncle Paul a half and GBD got the last half.

Why was the empty sack so important? Well this was the final act in the ceremony of eating cracked seed. We got to lick the inside of the package and that too was ONO!

Well one day we were playing jacks on the front porch of a home on Lusitana Street that Kekaa Boyd's father owned. Eddie, Walter, Uncle Paul, Maddie and Yvonne Boyd were playing and Kekaa had a package of cracked seed in one hand and playing jacks with the other. There was one piece of cracked seed protruding from the top of the bag and all eyes were fixed on that piece of candy. Well Kekaa was pretty selfish and never offered a piece of cracked seed to anyone. The torture was unbearable to sit there hoping for a piece but that little so and so never offered any. Nice kid.

DOUBLE ROPE WASN'T FIRST

One way to become famous or to make the record books is to be first at something, so people strive to be first so they can have their claim to fame. For example if someone like Thomas Edison invents something he is remembered for his invention. However, others can claim to be first and this could cause a problem. In the early days of invention, the first to the Patent Office was the winner. For example, the telephone was invented by Elisha Gray, but Alexander Graham Bell beat him to the Patent Office by thirty five minutes.

When Grandpa Bigdog and Uncle Paul were growing up we had a hero in Uncle Joe Carvalho. He was a dairyman, very physically strong man and usually had a simple solution to any complex problem. Uncle Paul and GBD spent a lot of time in the summers at Auntie Annie and Uncle Joe's place in Kailua. Uncle Joe had a dairy near Kaneohe and we used to go to the barn every chance we could to help out feeding the cows, cutting grass and cleaning the barn. Some of Uncle Joe's cows would kick when being milked so he usually carried a rope that he doubled to tie the cow's legs. As a result he earned the nickname "DOUBLE ROPE".

When we misbehaved Double Rope would threaten us that if we did not behave he would whack our legs with a Double Rope. As a result we referred to him more as Double Rope than Uncle Joe. That name was known all over Kailua.

If Double Rope had a problem with someone he would usually say that he would go after them with a double rope. [We could surely use some of his remedy in Washington today].

To illustrate Double Rope's simple solutions GBD remembers an incident when one of his large Holstein cows, Kukaiau, got caught in a barbed wire fence and cut an artery in her milk bag spewing blood all over the pasture. When Uncle Paul and I found her we brought her to the barn and Double Rope went to the feed room and collected a big handful of spider webs and plugged the artery and saved the cow's life. Double Rope died in 1964.

Uncle Paul and GBD always thought of Double Rope as a hero of sorts and that he was the first to use a double rope to solve complex problems. But, alas, someone beat him to the Patent Office. You see 2000 years ago Jesus used a Double Rope to cleanse the Temple. I wonder if Double Rope learned the art from Jesus?

Uncle Wally had a dream about Uncle Joe describing his death. Double Rope started up the long stairs to Heaven's Gate and rang the bell. St. Peter answered the door and had a big piece of chalk in his hand. St. Peter told Double Rope that he needed to go back down the stairs and write one sin on each step. After some time Double Rope rang the bell again. When St. Peter answered, Double Rope said, "**I NEED MORE CHALK**"

DOUBLE ROPE'S INGENUITY

When we lived in Honolulu, Uncle Paul and I used to spend a lot of time, especially in the summer at Double Rope's dairy. Uncle Joseph Carvalho was a dairyman and during our growing up we witnessed his activity as a dairyman. Double Rope was his nickname and he had a penchant for going bankrupt. But he really knew his business and was as strong as a mule.

There were many dairies around the other side of the Nuuanu Pali. The largest dairy, Eagle Rock Ranch, was owned by Lawrence Campos who milked several hundred cows a day. In Kaneohe Willie Salado and a man named Piper had sizable dairies. Double Rope's dairy was leased from H. K, Castle and it was situated at the junction of the Pali Road one branch going to Kaneohe and the other to Kailua and Lanikai. Double Rope had about 110 cows milking and it was a rough life.

For example, milking was done by hand and started at midnight and lasted till about 6 am. Then Double Rope had to deliver the milk to Honolulu at the Dairyman's Association near McKinley School. After recovering his milk cans, he would pick up a load of pineapple bran and oats and head back to the barn. Then it was off to cut hono hono grass for the cows. This meant we would take sickles and go to any field and cut grass and load it onto his 1934 Chevy truck to distribute to the cattle. Then it was home for some sleep and then off the barn at noon to milk again.

In addition to his double rope, Double Rope also carried a sickle for cutting grass. The dairy was at the bottom of a valley, one end being a banana patch and a swamp. To get to the barn there was a dirt road that had a bridge over a small creek. One day Double Rope went toward the swamp looking for a cow. The poor cow had delivered a calf but was stuck in the mud. So Double Rope took his sickle and cut guava branches and grass and made a platform so the cow could work her way out of the mud.

At the end of milking Walter or Uncle Wally would bottle up milk in quarts and we would deliver to customers in Kailua and Lanikai. Double Rope did not have refrigeration so he took his milk to Willie Salado's dairy to store overnight. Later Double Rope found out that Willie was siphoning off the butterfat to upgrade his own milk. So Larry Moore got Double Rope to build his own refrigerated milk room.

To get milk to the Dairymen's Association the farmers used a variety of trucks. Double Rope had a 1934 Chevy Stake Truck, Lawrence Campos bought two White Trucks from Schuman Carriage in Honolulu, and Piper had an old Faegol truck and Willie Salado an International.

So early in the morning Double Rope would load his truck with the milk cans. [He usually brought us a quart of milk and eggs.] Then he would drive slowly past the bullpen, over the wooden bridge, up the dirt road to the concrete highway. Then began the grueling climb up the Pali road. First was the intersection that led to Kaneohe then up the grade to the half way house then on to the hairpin turn. This was a tough turn since on the way up the grade rose steeply. Some people with Model T cars used to use reverse gear and back up, since reverse were stronger than first gear. When Double Rope finally reached the summit there was always a very strong wind blowing such that many rooftops of cars were blown away or tarps covering the milk cans.

One day Uncle Paul and I were standing on Nuuanu Street outside of our school and every car that passed by we would holler "UNCLE JOE" knowing full well that he drove a big blue truck. Well down the hill came this old Buick sedan and we yelled "UNCLE JOE" and much to our surprise it was Double Rope. His truck failed so he borrowed a car and tied milk cans down in the front and back seat and got his milk to town.

Another time he was driving home and Sonny distracted him and he hit a telephone pole and damaged the body of the truck. Double Rope got some strong rope and tied up the truck and got his milk to town. He later had the truck fixed at Date Service Station.

One day after a huge rainstorm the bridge was washed out and Double Rope could not drive out. Lucky there was a pickup truck near the barn so he loaded the milk cans and drove them to the creek, then carried the cans across the creek to the larger truck. Eventually her got a new bridge built and Double Rope continued with his dairy farming.

There are kuave trees in Hawaii that have long yellow beans that are sweet and the cows really like this. So Double Rope would drive down near Lanikai where there were groves of these trees and we would pick beans off the ground and fill gunnysacks with beans. Unfortunately, these trees drop large thorns and being barefooted we were always stepping on the thorns with unpleasant results. Good for the cows, bad for us.

MIOSAKE

Nuannu Pali Road

When Grandpa Bigdog was growing up in Hawaii he lived in Honolulu on the slopes of Punchbowl, an extinct volcano. Honolulu was a big city and we were thus city dwellers.

Enter Uncle Joe. Uncle Paul and I called Uncle Joe "Double Rope". He earned this title because he always told us boys that if we did not behave, he would take a double rope and whack us on the legs.

Uncle Joe was a real tough guy and strong as a horse. He owned a dairy on the other side of the Pali. (The Pali is a high mountain peak that divides the island of Oahu in two). On the other side of the Pali, Uncle Joe had his dairy where he milked about 130 cows twice a day.

Uncle Paul and I used to love to go to the dairy and watch the cows. Eventually, GBD learned how to milk cows and got so good that one day I milked 36 cows, all by hand.

Uncle Joe had a mixture of cows. There were Holstein cows that are large black and white cows that give lots of milk. He also had Guernsey cows that were red and white and Jersey cows which were fawn colored and small cows, about five feet high.

Uncle Joe's barn was near a swamp and we had to be sure that the cows did not go into the swamp and drink the water because of liver flukes in the swamp water.

Enter Miosake!!

Uncle Joe did business with a Japanese man named Miosake (Miosake). He lived near Kahuku and his cows were also near a swamp. He would come over and try to sell cows to Uncle Joe and Uncle Joe would usually buy a cow from him. Unfortunately, after a few weeks the poor cow died from liver flukes and Miosake couldn't figure why the cow died.

One day Uncle Paul and GBD were playing near the barn when we saw a big Packard car coming down the dirt road leading to Uncle Joe's barn. We quickly ran to the barn and told Uncle Joe that Miosake had driven into the barnyard. When we went back out, there was Miosake in his Packard car with a Jersey bull in the back seat. He proceeded to pull the bull out of the car and walk him over to "Double Rope".

"Look Joe", Miosake said, "I got a nice bull to sell you.

Uncle Joe laughed at Miosake. "Look at my big cows and you bring me a small Jersey bull?" No sale.

So Miosake opened the door of his Packard and started loading the bull into the back seat. Uncle Paul and I were on one end pulling the rope and Miosake was behind the bull pushing him back into the car.

Can you just imagine what that looked like…the poor bull was so confused and Miosake lost a sale.

EDDIE'S TAXI RIDE

We learn at church and school that Purgatory is a real place where many souls must go before they can go to heaven. Well, this is not necessarily true, because I think that Eddie and I have already been there. Going to Cathedral School was as close to Purgatory as we will ever get, with the likes of Brother Leo, Brother Eugene and Brother Leonard.

To illustrate, we should remember how Eddie and I used to have to dodge flying erasers from Brother Leo and how Paul got more F grades than anyone else.

When we were in the eighth grade we had Brother Eugene for our teacher. He was also the Principal at this school and ruled with an iron fist, since that was the only way he could control the inmates of that school.

One of the toughest subjects was math. I can remember we had to multiply large numbers such as 478 x 963. This took a while to figure out, but we had about 10 of these to do for homework. Well, Jonnie Medeiros had figured a way out. Jonnie had good handwriting and his papers were very neat. So he would look up the answers in the back of the book and write the correct answer down. He would then fill in any numbers he wanted to make it look like he had done the calculation. So I decided to try Jonnie's trick, but my handwriting was so poor I could not fudge my way past anything.

Well, Brother Eugene caught me and sent me to the office for 10 whacks with the ruler for not doing my homework the right way.

Enough of Purgatory!

The way Eddie and I got relief was to get on our bikes after school and ride around instead of doing our homework.

One evening, after dinner, we got on our bikes and began to cruise around Lusitana Street. Eddie had his famous bike with the knee action and he was always faster than me, so I was pedaling hard to keep up with him. His bike's fancy knee action made riding over bumps easy.

So after riding around for a while, we headed down Kuakini Street and over toward Kawananakoa School. Eddie went roaring down the sidewalk on Kuakini Street with me in close pursuit, and then we turned up Fort Street. Eddie was looking back and waving me on to catch up to him. Just then Eddie turned a sharp left into an alley and head on into a taxicab! The knee action on his bike hit Eddie in the seat and propelled him onto the hood of the taxi and Eddie was thrashing his arms in all directions.

I ran my bike onto some grass and rolled over laughing so hard at Eddie swimming on the hood of the taxi. The taxi driver, a woman, was furious and really shaken up.

Well, the first thing Eddie did was to check his tires to make sure the wheels were not wobbling. We then picked up our bikes and rode off.

EXECUTIVE STAFF

When Grandpa Bigdog lived in Honolulu, there were a number of dairies on the island of Oahu. One of the biggest dairies was Campos Dairy that was owned by Lawrence Campos and it was called Eagle Rock Ranch because there was a large lava outcrop in the middle of a flat field shaped like an eagle. Near this rock was a very tall coconut tree that seemed to stretch out forever. The Campos dairy had two White trucks that hauled milk to Honolulu everyday. Cousin Peter Carvalho worked for Campos dairy and GBD used to go there to help milk cows and drive the cows in toward the barn.

Other dairies on the other side of the Pali included Julian Jama's, Willie Salado, Piper and of course Double Rope. (Uncle Paul and I called Uncle Joe Double Rope). Uncle Joe had a large dairy that he rented from Harold Castle and it was located below the fork in the road that led on the left to Kaneohe and to the right to Kailua and Waimanalo and Lanikai.

Double Rope had over a hundred milking cows and this took a lot of work to milk them twice a day especially milking was done by hand and that took a lot of time and manpower. As a result, Double Rope had to hire an executive staff to assist with the milking. Cousin Walter worked for Double Rope who had to recruit additional executives. Double Rope would pay some of these executives Room and Board and GBD can remember some of them sleeping over in Auntie Annie's house in Kailua. In addition, there was a long house on the dairy property with several apartments and Double Rope could put up his executives in these apartments.

Most of these executives were never in danger of winning the Nobel Prize and some of them were real characters. GBD can remember two of them who stood out. One was a guy we called Barriga who had a huge beer

41

belly that stuck out over his belt. It was a wonder he could ever get close enough to milk a cow.

The other was a guy we knew as Cutchee who lived in one of the apartments on the dairy grounds. Cutchee was a lazy guy and Double Rope had to keep prodding him to get the cows milked. I think his first name was Manuel.

One of the interesting things Cutchee did to supplement his executive compensation was to go out to collect bottles. During the depression, one could get one or two cents for a coke or milk bottle. So in his spare time, Cutchee would drive his old truck around looking for bottles. What was so amusing to Uncle Paul and GBD was to see Cutchee driving up the Pali Road and stopping his truck if he spotted a reflection of a bottle at the bottom of a ravine. He would climb or actually slide down through the guava bushes to retrieve a bottle only to find out that the bottle was broken or worthless. He spent more money driving around looking for bottles than he made on bottle refunds.

But after all, some of the things executives do really doesn't make too much sense.

FEATURED SPEAKER

When Grandpa Bigdog was a student at Campbell High, he had lots of friends like Kent Clark, Mac Martin, CD Cutting, Frutie, Bob Hall, Albert Evans, Larry Lewis, Ray Flagg, Merrill Grim, Frank Smith and Jerry Finch, to name a few.

Ray Flagg was a very interesting guy!

Ray was a talented artist that did the art work for Paul J. Meyer during the Close Election and his creativity just abounded. Ray and I also worked at Drew's Cannery in the summer that provided us with some needed income. When we worked as pie boys during the canning season one summer, we did the night shift that ran from 5 pm to 5 am. After work Ray and I would walk home together. I lived on Foote Street near the cannery so I was home very quickly, but Ray lived on Apricot Avenue next to Sharon Wright and had a longer walk home.

Usually, when we got to the corner of Foote Street and Campbell Avenue we would launch into a long conversation about the stars, life in general and our big plans for the future. We would also have long discussions about developing a perpetual motion machine and how we could make one work. We also spent hours trying to figure out how to walk on water. [Years later Ray's youngest brother Rodger invented and patented such a device].

Ray eventually bought a Ford four door convertible and we used to ride around town with Sharon Wright and Nancy Allen whenever he had enough money to buy gasoline that was rationed.

One of the interesting things we did in high school at the beginning of the year was to have a picture taken for the yearbook. With the picture we got a sheet of pictures about 2x3 that fit in a wallet. It was fun to exchange pictures especially with the girls. As a result I had a number of pictures of Nina Page, Dolores Woods, Gayle Smith and others. There are consequences that can follow one having these pictures, an example follows.

Campbell High had a large main building, an Auditorium and a smaller classroom building facing Winchester Boulevard. Behind the main building was a large Gym facing north and south. At the south end, closest to the main building was the girl's locker room; the boy's locker was located at the north end. The girls who did not participate in gym on any particular day would congregate on the steps of the gym.

Well, one day Ray and I were in the boy's locker room when we were summoned to the office. So Coach Walt Hill told us to go to the office. As we walked along Ray was going through my wallet looking at my girl pictures when he asked me who a certain girl was and I said:

"Oh, that's Dolores Woods. She's got a big ass!!"

Well, as we turned the corner all the girls were looking to see the featured speaker. Poor Ray and I had to walk about 100 more feet to the main building with no cover. So be careful what you say in public.

FRED WRIGHT'S COMING

When Grandpa Bigdog was a young boy, I lived in Honolulu near my good friend Eddie Medeiros. We spent a lot of time riding bikes, hitching rides on buses and trying to get ripe mangos from the trees.

Life in Honolulu was really city style and a sharp contrast from the country. Uncle Paul and I used to like to go to Auntie Annie's place in Kailua on the other side of the island because there were a lot of fun things we could do like hunting for coconuts or climbing coconut trees to pick the green coconuts. These were very delicious, especially since they were full of coconut water and very sweet. When we cracked open the shells of green coconuts we could scoop out the coconut meat with a piece of coconut shell. Another favorite food was guavas that we were always on the lookout for; green or ripe.

Perhaps the greatest fun was going to Double Rope's dairy and every afternoon, just after noon, you could hear Double Rope starting up his truck getting ready to go to the dairy. Once in a while Sonny would be high up in a coconut tree and hearing the truck start would fly down the tree and run for the truck with Double Rope and cousin Walter waiting for us kids to climb onto the back of the truck.

Running a dairy was a tough job. Poor Double Rope would milk cows from midnight to five in the morning, come home to sleep a bit, eat breakfast and take the milk to Honolulu to Dairymen's Association where he sold the milk. Then he would load up pineapple bran and oats and head back to Kailua. Then he and the rest of us would go out to cut hono-hono grass for the cows and drop it off in the pasture.

One of Double Rope's problems was Fred Wright. Fred Wright was the Inspector for the government and he checked on the sanitation and other possible health problems associated with producing safe milk products. Fred Wright lived in Papakolea just above the famous graveyards on Awaiolimu Street. He was a tough guy and gave Double Rope lots of trouble.

For example, he would check the foot washer, the milk room and the cleanliness of the barn. One of the rules that he really gave Double Rope trouble on was having calves in the barn. What Double Rope used to do when he had young calves was to milk the cow incompletely, then bring the calves to finish the job. This made it easier to feed calves then pouring milk into a bucket and trying to get the calves to drink. As a result, Double Rope always had Uncle Paul and GBD watching for Fred Wright.

One day we were busy with milking and did not pay much attention to the entry road that came off the Pali Road, across a creek and into the dairy yard. Uncle Paul, Sonny and GBD were dragging calves into the barn when someone yelled: FRED WRIGHT IS COMING!

Double Rope yelled at us to get the calves out of the barn, but the calves were pretty stubborn and we had a heck of a time pulling them past the fence by the foot washer. Well, when Fred showed up we still had two calves in the barn and poor Double Rope caught heck again from Fred Wright.

So watch out for Fred Wright.

FREE CANDY

When Grandpa Bigdog lived in Honolulu we lived on the slopes of Punchbowl. This is a large crater situated right in the center of the city. One of the values of this was all the steep hills which made for great skating, bike riding and for running skate cars.

Near our home on Boyd lane was a grocery store run by two Chinese men and it was called HO CHIN LEE store. One of the attractions was a large case in the front of the store that contained candy. Now candy to us was such items as cracked seed, sweet and sour semoi (dried plum) mango seed, preserved olives that we called footballs because of the shape and sawa seed, a very salty form of dried plum. All of these were stored in large glass jars sitting on top of the candy counter and some inside the counter. These were mouthwatering treats unavailable to us, since we had no money to buy them.

Rich kids like Maddie and Kekaa Boyd (rich because they could afford to buy a sack of semoi) were the envy of Uncle Paul and I. What was real torture was to stand in front of those candy jars and drool. Once in a while we could come up with a nickel and were able to buy a sack of semoi (preserved plum). This was a real treasure and we relished that treat.

One of the facts we knew living in Hawaii was that we were going to have a war with Japan and the natives there had no doubt that it would happen. Also we used to have practice blackout drills to test our ability to darken the island in case of an air raid.

Now, because of this impending disaster, it was easy to dream up a solution to getting some free candy. Uncle Paul, Eddie Medeiros and GBD used to talk about this all the time. We figured that if there was a war, the Japanese would bomb the store and we could then pick up free semoi. This was not a bad idea in that kid thinking is not very good.

So along came December 7, 1941 and the bombs flew and the whole island was chaos. They did not bomb the store, but if they had it would not have done us much good. You see, on December 8, there was martial law imposed on the islands and they announced over the radio that anyone caught looting would be shot.

Well that certainly took care of our **free candy.**

FRUIT COCKTAIL

When Grandpa Bigdog was in high school we lived in Campbell, California near Drew's Cannery. This cannery was later sold to Hunt's Foods and continued to package fruit. The fruit-canning season went something like this. Apricots were the first crop to be canned, then when peaches and pears came along the cannery would can peaches, pears and make fruit cocktail.

Students always looked forward to getting summer employment at the cannery and eagerly awaited the opening of the canning season. One problem was the union. In order to work at the cannery we had to join the union, pay dues and receive the benefits of higher wages. The union representative was Lou Genaci who also ran the steam boilers for the cannery.

Well one summer it appears that the cannery did not want to package apricots so the union called a strike. (Probably a little collusion between labor and management). So we did not get summer employment during the apricot season. So the farmers had to dry their apricots.

At the end of the apricot season the strike was miraculously resolved and we got hired to work canning peaches. With GBD's skill as a Pie Boy, I was gainfully employed again. The procedure was essentially the same as with apricots, except that peaches need to be peeled. Peaches were sawed in two, the pits removed then peeled by dipping them in hot lye to remove the fuzz. The ladies sorted the good peach halves and the not so good ones (size or shape) were designated for fruit cocktail. And the pits would go into a separate tub to be dispensed like the apricot pits were onto the waste conveyer.

Fruit cocktail was made from diced pears and peaches, Thompson seedless grapes and maraschino cherries. Peaches that were not fit for halves or sliced were carried up on a conveyer to a hopper and dropped into a dicing machine consisting of a rectangular pattern of steel blades that diced the fruit. The big problem was pits. If a pit got into the dicing machine it would shatter the blades and shut down the dicer until new blades could be installed. This was costly and stopped the production line.

Well sure enough here was Mrs. Silva again at her station alert to an occasional peach pit. And of course history repeats itself and GBD dumped a pan of peach pits onto the wrong conveyer. Before I could run to where she was the pits were overwhelming her efforts to remove them and sure enough they went into the dicer and ruined the dicer.

Lucky for GBD I did not get fired and the next summer I got a job as an electrician so I did not have to do the mentally challenging job of being a Pie Boy.

GOODNIGHT!!

When Grandpa Bigdog lived in Honolulu, our family attended Our Lady of Peace Church on Fort Street. Later on the church built a new church on Pauoa Street nearer our home on Boyd Lane. This church was named Blessed Sacrament Church.

Grandpa Bigdog was an altar boy at this church and Fr. Gregory Rotier was our priest. A number of my friends were also altar boys. There were Peter Gomez and his brother, and Joe Keenee a Hawaiian boy who lived on the slopes of Punchbowl in a very small house, just up the street from Boogo on Puowaina Drive. GBD can remember that Joe's father used to plant sweet potatoes in their garden.

Well, one day poor Joe's parents died and Joe had to go live with his uncle on Nuuanu Avenue.

One of the many tasks altar boys had to do at Blessed Sacrament Church was to serve at 7:30 mass in the morning and to serve at Sunday masses. This was done by rotation so that everyone got a chance to serve. We also served at Holy Hour and during lent on Friday night for the Stations of the Cross. This was usually at 7 in the evening and lasted about an hour.

Now, back to Joe Keenee. GBD mentioned that Joe went to live with his uncle. His uncle was the caretaker of the cemetery on Nuuanu Avenue near the hill where Eddie Medeiros had the accident with the sewer covers. This cemetery was a large place and Joe's uncle lived at the far back of the cemetery.

One night GBD was serving at the Stations of the Cross with Joe Kee-nee and Peter Gomez and some other boys. After the service Joe asked GBD if he wanted to go out and play before curfew. (There was a nine o'clock curfew in Honolulu and we all had to be off the streets when the siren sounded at the Aloha Tower).

So GBD agreed to go with Joe, but he told GBD that he had to stop by his house to get something before we could go out to play. Well we walked over to Nuuanu Avenue then up to the entrance to the cemetery and it was now pitch dark. In order to get to Joe's uncle's home we had to walk diagonally through the cemetery to the very end. It was real scary and Joe kept mentioning how scared he was. When we finally reached the end of the cemetery, there was a large hibiscus hedge surrounding the house. Joe disappeared into the hedge and said, "Goodnight".

What Joe had done was to trick me into walking home with him, because he was afraid of walking through the cemetery alone.

Now what?

GBD was really scared and began walking back toward Nuuanu Avenue and tripping over gravestones. Finally, GBD walked across the cemetery to a side street, climbed the stone wall there and made it to a dark street. From there GBD ran as fast as he could till he reached Nuuanu Avenue and safety.

That was sure a dirty trick to play on another altar boy and one GBD will never forget.!

HAOLE GIRLS

Grandpa Bigdog lived on Boyd Lane in Honolulu near Eddie Medeiros house on Lusitana Street and on the slopes of Punchbowl volcano. The roads were quite steep, especially Holy Ghost Hill. Another rather steep street was San Antonio Street that angled down from Pouwaina Drive to Lusitana Street. Around that corner Awaiolimu Street angled into Lusitana Street. At that point there was a house with a large front porch and that became the focus of an interesting tale of cowardice and courage.

There was not too much going on around San Antonio Street. Alex Vierra, one of our cousins, lived on this street that was also a shortcut to getting up to Punchbowl. Alex was very kind to us and bought bread for us. Every afternoon a Krispy Krust delivery truck would show up and deliver bread, still warm from the oven.

Generally, nothing happened at this end of San Antonio Street until one day something unusual happened. Two very pretty haole girls moved in. Their family had come from the mainland and found a house at the corner of San Antonio and Lusitana Street.

These very pretty girls used to spend a part of the afternoon sitting on the front porch of their home. Soon a bunch of the local boys began to show up like flies on a fresh pile of cow manure. Frank Yamani, Pig (Gilbert Diaz), Ah-ba-gee, Eddie Medeiros, Uncle Paul, GBD, Johnnie and Walter Medeiros, Guava, Willie Olivera, to name a few began congregating across the street to watch these haole girls.

The next thing we knew the guys began to show off to get the girls attention. Some would climb up the telephone pole, while others would ride their bikes up and down San Antonio Street and do all kind of funny things to get their attention. The rest of us would sit around and play games like knife or a marble game, all the while keeping an eager eye on that front porch.

One of the most unusual things about this gang of suitors was their cowardice. No one had the courage to go across the street to talk directly to these pretty girls, figuring that their antics would gain them some fame. So every afternoon the crowd of admirers would show up and go through their paces, some even getting into fights over a good viewing position along the roadside. Then came a big shock!

One afternoon while the crowd gathered for their usual afternoon staring and show off session, Snookie DeRego shows up. He lived up on Pouwaina Drive and had not been a regular participant in the daily foolishness. Instead of joining in the antics, he shocked everyone by boldly walking across the street right up to the porch and started a conversation with the two girls.

A lot of jaws dropped! What was Snookie doing?

Well, Snookie got a date with one of the girls and the next afternoon he took her to the Hawaii Theater to a movie. Snookie and the girl headed down Lusitana Street and walked over to the theater with a full entourage of stunned followers a safe distance behind the two. The few who had enough money to buy a ticket followed then into the theater and took up their positions behind the couple. After the movie they followed them home, still stunned that Snookie had the courage to do the unthinkable…walking across the street to talk with the haole girls.

HAU

One of the things Uncle Paul and GBD used to do when we were growing up in Hawaii was climbing trees. This is a fun thing to do and we climbed many trees. The only real hazard was the chance of falling out of the tree. Here are some tree climbing events:

We used to climb guava trees to get to the ripe guavas, the best of which were always high up and hardest to pick. Mango trees were another favorite, but they were usually big trees and difficult or dangerous to climb. So to get mangos we would throw rocks at the trees hoping to knock off a mango. Uncle Wally came up with a metal loop attached to a long stick. He attached a cloth bag to the loop and we could reach up to the mangos and shake them into the bag.

Another favorite tree to climb was the coconut tree. Auntie Annie had some small trees in the empty lot on the makai side of her yard and GBD was able to climb up and get some nice coconuts. But the tall trees were another matter, since we were not strong enough to climb these. But cousin Sonny was very strong and he could shinny up the tree and knock coconuts down for us. The only trouble was that by the time he got to the top of the tree he would grab the first branch and pull himself up into the tree. But one day he did just that and the branch gave way. Sonny came crashing down onto a barbed wire fence and really go hurt.

There were others like the mountain apple and the papaya trees. These trees like the coconut are hard to climb since there are no branches to support us. Another tree that you really couldn't climb was the koa bush. This was a small tree with tiny leaves and no strong branches. These grow all around Punchbowl. One day we were watching a motorcycle hill climb on Punchbowl. The path up the slope was lined with koa trees and we stood around watching the bikes go up the hill. Uncle Paul decided to do one better and climbed up a koa tree. Since these are small he bunched three of them together so they would hold him and he got a birds eye view of the action. He was showing off to us until a motorcycle came roaring up the slope out of control and right for Uncle Paul who was now hanging on for dear life. Luck for him the bike missed him.

Our favorite tree though was the Hau tree (pronounced How). This tree, a member of the hibiscus family has many branches and spreads out a great distance so that we could climb to the to top easily. There are so many branches that you cannot fall out of the tree and get hurt since the intertwining branches broke our fall.

There was a large Hau tree on Oneawa Street just about a half mile from the Coconut Grove Club at a bend in the road. We used to spend hours in that tree telling stories and watching the horses in the yard across from the tree.

One day Auntie Annie ran out of kerosene and sent Uncle Paul and GBD to buy some so she could cook dinner for the Double Rope and the dairy hands who boarded there. Well we got the kerosene but on the way home we stopped at the Hau tree and met some friends and forgot that we had to get back home with the kerosene. After spending a lot of time talking and laughing, we set off for Auntie Annie's house with the kerosene.

Boy did she give us heck and rightfully so!

ICE HOUSE

The other day it was quite warm and Carol and I finished our yard work and then headed for the swimming pool off our patio. That brought to mind our formative years when we used to want to go swimming but had no swimming pool.

When Uncles Wally, Paul and I lived on Awaiolimu Street in Honolulu there was a small stream behind the house. Pauoa Stream. This stream did not have any good swimming holes so we used to pile rock and make a dam so we could obtain a three-foot deep swimming hole. There was a lot of limu (algae) in the stream so we used limu to patch leaks in the dam.

There were better swimming holes, but they were on Nuannu Stream. Nuannu stream had four great swimming holes. Down near the cemetery was a Fraga pond that was not too deep, but was great for younger kids. [This was the place that had an old stagnant pool that Eddie Medieros rode his bike on and fell in]. The next great pond was Alikoki that was deeper and where we did most of our swimming because it was close to the Ice House. To get to Alikoki we had to cross through a fence at Iolani High School's football practice field. Alikoki had two good diving spots; a low one and a higher one about fifteen feet above the water. One day Uncle Wally dived into the pond and disappeared. After a few minutes we got scared and were getting ready to call for help. After 10 minutes he came back to the surface. He had found an old lava tube and swam into it. The lava tube led to a storm drain and he could see daylight. That sure gave us a scare.

The next pond was Lilly Pond further up the trail. On the other side of this pond was a large lava tube with Hawaiian pteroglyphs scratched on the walls. There was also a fountain near Lilly Pond and we always drank from it. Further up was Kapana Pond the deepest and more difficult pond to swim in. I never swam in that pond. Uncle Wally was the only one who did high dives from there.

It was always so hot in Honolulu in the summer time so we always made sure that after swimming we walked over to the Ice House. The Honolulu Sake Brewery was located near Alikoki and in addition to making ice they brewed saki. On the loading dock they always had an ice cooler with paper cups for their workers. We always sneaked onto the dock and got our fill of ice water that helped on the long trek home.

We never had swimming suits so we used to designate a look out to keep watch in case any girls showed up. Once in a while we would be swimming naked when a group of girls seemed to appear out of nowhere and that caused a real problem. Another problem was when some kids went swimming we would tie their pants in knots so when the girls showed up and they rushed for their pants they couldn't get them on in time.

LIBERTY THEATER

When I lived in Honolulu going to the theater was a real luxury. There were many theaters in downtown Honolulu like the King, Queen, Liberty and Roosevelt. The Roosevelt was Uncles Paul and Wally's favorite since it only cost a dime and they ran cowboy movies and B rated pictures like the Mummy's Tomb and the Werewolf.

The summer after the Pearl Harbor bombing, I found a job at the Liberty Theater as an usher and this was my first big time job paying real money. This was short lived since in September 1942 we moved to California and that put a halt to my big income.

We settled in Campbell that had a theater of the same name and I learned to become a projectionist. This was my ticket to college as I was able to pay my way while working full time at the Campbell Theater and later at the Sunnyvale Theater.

One of my good friends in high school was Ray Flagg. Ray was a good artist and loved cars. He and I were pie boys at Drew's Cannery and we worked the night shift from 5 pm to 5 am. After work we would walk home and talk about our futures. Usually the stars were out and we would wonder about the universe. So we would stand on the corner of Foote Street and Campbell Avenue and talk for awhile then he would head off for his home on Apricot Street.

One of the students at Campbell High told us about seeing a burlesque show in San Francisco and he drew a good audience as he explained his exciting visit to the Liberty Burlesque. So Ray and I discussed the issue. At that time there were some famous stars [?] like Blaze Starr, Tempest Storm and others who toured the Burlesque circuit. So Ray and I planned a secret visit to SF after reading in the SF newspaper that the Liberty was featuring the Queen of Sheba.

One evening we drove in my 1934 Ford to SF to check out the Queen. We got lost in the big city and ran down a one way street and nearly hit a taxi. Finally we found the Liberty and went in. They were showing a foreign movie with a terrible sound track that we couldn't understand. Then after the movie they turned the lights on sold popcorn and Ray and I proceeded to get a seat in the front row, center stage. After a few comedy acts the Queen was next and we were glued to our seats.

When the music started, out came the Queen of Sheba, a belly dancer about 45 years old with long black hair dancing across the stage. This was great until she smiled. She had a front tooth missing and that did it for us. We scurried out as fast as we could and kept reassuring each other on the way home that we would not tell anyone.

MOTORCYCLE HILL CLIMB

When Grandpa Bigdog was growing up in Honolulu, we did a lot of funny things. An interesting experience was to watch a motorcycle hill climb.

This event required some steep hills and a few men who must have had a screw loose somewhere. The hills were located in two places that GBD remembers. One was at the intersection of the Pali Road where the road turned to Kailua on the right and Kaneohe on the left. The hill was on the mauka side of Double Ropes's dairy that he rented from Harold Castle. The other was on Punchbowl on the way to Papakolea on Puowaina Drive.

This site was easily reached from our home on Awaiolimu Street. All we had to do was to walk up the street, go through the Chinese cemetery and cross Pouwaina Drive. The slopes of Punchbowl crater are very steep and perfect for hill climbing. There was a dirt lane running up the side of the mountain and the edges of the lane were lined with pinenee (cactus) and koa trees. Now the koa trees were really no trees, but overgrown weeds. These are thin, about one inch in diameter and have no big branches but grow closely together. Climbing a koa tree is impossible. The only good function of a grove of koa trees is to save Uncle Paul when he tried to commit suicide by running Uncle Wally's wagon off the stonewall.

To do a hill climb, the ding-dong on the motorcycle would have chains on the rear wheel for more traction and had a leather strap tied to the ignition key that would allow the rider to jerk the key out at the end of the climb to keep him from being run over by the motorcycle. The rider would gun the engine and roar up the side of Punchbowl to see how far up he could ride. Whoever reached to top would win. Unfortunately not all riders were

61

that lucky and many lost control and roared off into the koa trees or the pinenees with pretty bad results.

One day we heard there was going to be a hill climb, so Uncle Paul, Wally and GBD headed up to Punchbowl. A number of our friends were there, Edwin Sousa, Harold and Gilbert Dias, Sonny Ornelas and others. It was hard to get a good viewing spot, so we crowded along the sides of the lane hoping to see the motorcycles.

Uncle Paul decided to outsmart everyone, so he climbed halfway up the slope and climbed a koa tree by using several koa trees to give him support. He began to tease us because he had the best view, which he did.

Pretty soon there came a motorcycle roaring up the slope, the driver lost control and guess what? He was heading right for Uncle Paul in the koa trees. Lucky for Uncle Paul, the motorcycle stopped before he hit the koa trees and Uncle Paul was spared a trip to Queen's Hospital.

MARY BROWN'S FATHER

When I first came to California in 1942, our family moved in with my Grandfather Manuel Miranda in the small town of Campbell. We lived on the other side of the tracks in this town that was the center of the fruit growing and processing industry. Santa Clara Valley was strewn with apricot, peach, prune and cherry ranches where each family could operate about five to ten acres of fruit.

To process the fruit there was Drew's Cannery and Hyde's Dehydrator. My uncle Joe Carvalho had such a ranch with apricot and prune trees. At harvest time many sold their fruit to Drew's Cannery or to Hydes's Dehydrator, but many farmers would simply dry their prunes or apricots in the sun; a laborious task.

I and many of my friends like Ray Flagg, Kent Clark and Mac Martin worked summer jobs at Drew's or Hydes and that was a good source of income.

Since Campbell was a small town few had telephones but we did have a highly effective communication center at the Campbell Shoe Shop. Tony and his dad ran the place repairing shoes. In addition to repairing shoes Tony had two shoe shining chairs that were elevated and four chairs where customers could sit or kids like us could drop in and talk with Tony.

Tony knew everything that was going on in town and news of note appeared to emanate from the shoe shop, then to Tony Rafanti's Bar then on down to Murray's Bar. So if you needed good information or some gossip Tony's was the place to start.

One day one of Campbell's Nobel laureates decided to drop in to have a chat with Tony because it did not matter if he was shining shoes, since he would just go on with the shoe shining and carry on a conversation. So this Nobel laureate starts bragging to Tony that he had a date with Mary Brown that night. Then he began to discuss some of the great attributes of Mary in unacceptable language and his game plan for the exciting evening activities.

Meanwhile, Tony was trying to change the topic by bringing up the Kingfish and his antics, while shining his customer's shoes with great fervor as if he was trying to finish and get his customer on his way. Meanwhile, the laureate kept describing what his plans for the evening were.

After the customer left, Tony made a brief statement:

"That was Mary Brown's Dad!!"

MY TURN, MY TURN

When Grandpa Bigdog lived in Hawaii, he had a lot of things to keep him busy. We used to make skate cars, sleds to ride down Punchbowl and made sling shots to practice target shooting. We also used to make rifles from wood and then cut large rubber bands from old tire tubes so we could shoot the rubber 'bullets' when we played Cowboy and Indian.

Another great activity for Uncle Paul and GBD was to go to Auntie Annie's house in Kailua. Auntie Annie lived in the coconut grove on a large lot. There were a lot of things to do at Auntie Anne's place. She had a chicken coop about where cousin Walter's home is now, a duck pen and a pig pen. On the makai side (Hawaiian for toward the ocean) of the yard was the pigpen and she had a big black pig in the pen. In front of the pigpen and closer to Hualani Street there were some cows tied to coconut trees. Cousin Peter had a big black cow, Babe, and he was the only one who could milk her. At times there were some calves that Uncle Paul and GBD fed.

Over by the duck pen there were some banana plants and they usually had large stalks of bananas. We never were without bananas.

Also scattered around the yard was an old Buick car that did not run anymore and over toward the pigpen was the real favorite of Uncle Paul and GBD. It was an old Willys-Knight that had been converted to a pickup truck and was now abandoned. This was where we spent hours driving this old klunker.

This old truck had some switches that we could turn on and off and the clutch was soft enough for us to depress and shift the gears. So we would sit behind the wheel and drive this truck all over Kailua (even though it was up on blocks). So we would fight over who was going to drive then pretend we were backing up to Hualani street then off to the Pali. Then we would shift gears as we passed halfway house, hairpin turn and other land marks up the Pali Road. The trouble was GBD couldn't get too far with out Uncle Paul yelling at me, "MY TURN, MY TURN". I would try my best to fend him off, but eventually had to give up the wheel so he could drive.

Then he would make a lot of noise, WROOOM, WROOM, as he drove the old pickup over to Waimanalo and over toward Koko Head. Meanwhile, GBD was struggling to get MY TURN. We spent many hours in that old jalope and really enjoyed turning the wheel and playing with the light switch and shifting gears.

We must have put thousands of miles on that old truck, but I can still see that old wreck sitting in the yard and Uncle Paul and GBD fighting over whose turn it was to drive.

MY TURN! MY TURN!

PIE BOY

FRUIT PACKING STATION

When Grandpa Bigdog moved from Honolulu to Campbell, California he decided to find some work in this small prune-apricot town. His first executive position was in retailing at the local Sprouse-Reitz 5 & 10 cent store where he swept the floor and kept the warehouse in order at a whopping salary of 25 cents/hour.

As GBD got older he was able to use his executive talent in the Food Processing Industry. Across the railroad tracks on Foote Street stood Drew's Cannery. They processed apricots, then peaches, pears and fruit cocktail in the summer and spinach in the fall. GBD's executive position was Pie Boy. Mac Martin, Roy Zimmer, Lawrence Hartley, Jerry Finch, Ray Flagg and Bob Hall also held various executive positions at Drew's Cannery and worked the night shift

In canning apricots, the apricots are moved about on conveyer belts to rows of pitting stands where women would pit the apricots and feed the apricot halves to another series of sinks where women washed and sorted the apricot halves and separated the fruit from pits. Halves that were not suited for canning were set aside in pans and placed on conveyers by the Pie Boy where they were packaged for pie apricots used by bakeries and food preparation kitchens. Another conveyer carried the pits to garbage from which the pits were sent to a recovery plant in Los Gatos where Jack Vitale worked. As the ladies filled these pans with apricots or pits, it was time for executives like GBD to dump the pans onto the proper conveyer.

GBD worked the night shift that starts at 6 pm and ran to 6 am. The ladies were quite bossy and disrespective to the Pie Boy executives and usually gave us a hard time. As the evening wore on it was easy to get tired and sleepy and one could lose control of the sequence of dumping the correct pan in the correct conveyer. In order to prevent an occasional pit from being mixed with the good apricots, a woman was seated next to the elevator conveyer to remove any stray pits. On the night shift this task was done by Mrs. Silva who was the wife of the night foreman, Joseph whose brother Frank Silva, we used to call him Fluffy because of his thick hair, was the Plant Superintendent.

The job of watching for stray pits did not require a high IQ and was surrounded with extreme boredom. It was interesting to watch Mrs. Silva, half asleep picking an occasional pit from the moving belts. All is well so long as the Pie Boys did their jobs.

Drew Canning Company, Campbell, California

Well, one night about 3 am, GBD was working his way along the aisles picking up pans and dumping them onto the proper conveyer, when he took a pan full of pits and dumped them onto the conveyer containing good apricots. For a few seconds GBD stood there watching the pile of pits move downstream before he realized what he had done. Suddenly GBD ran down the aisle toward Mrs. Silva just as the pits reached her sleepy post. She began to frantically pull pits from the conveyer, but was soon overwhelmed and had to push the emergency stop for all the conveyer belts. The maintenance crew came running over and Ross Borelli, the foreman proceeded to chewing GBD out for screwing up.

Unfortunately, GBD would have an opportunity to repeat this fiasco later on during Peach Season (See Fruit Cocktail)

PINEENEES

When Grandpa Bigdog lived in Honolulu, we lived on the slopes of Punchbowl, a volcanic tuff crater that was quite steep and covered with grass, koa trees and pineeenes. What we called pineenees is actually prickly pear cactus with long spikes and when blooming the flowers are very pretty. These flowers eventually become prickly pears that have tiny bristles that penetrate the skin and are very difficult to remove. As a result, we stayed away from these plants. Uncle Wally told us that the pears are really delicious but difficult to harvest.

Uncle Wally was a Boy Scout and as part of his camping training he had learned how to harvest these pears and proceeded to instruct GBD and Uncle Paul in the skill.

To harvest a prickly pear Uncle Wally would take a sharp stick cut from a koa tree (a member of the acacia family) and stick it into the top of the pear. Then he would take his pocketknife and cut the pear from the cactus leaf. The next step was critical because of the sharp barbs on the pear. He would then grab the pear with the thumb and middle finger at each end then slice into the skin along the long axis. Then holding the pear by the stick Uncle Wally cut off the other end of the pear and pried open the outer skin then reached in and pulled the pear core out. It is delicious. So that is all there was to this.

So one day Uncle Paul, GBD, Guava (Ah-Ba-Gee's brother) and Pig (Gilbert Dias) were climbing Punchbowl and we noticed that there were a lot of ripe pears on the pineenees. Uncle Paul remembered Uncle Wally's discourse on harvesting these so we set about to gather a few as instructed by our mentor. Well we were able to get three pears down to the ground with Uncle Paul directing the operation. After opening the pear he reached in to carefully grab the core. His work was that of an expert, working slowly with iron nerves until Uncle Paul's knife slipped and the pear shell snapped back spewing the core with bristles. He then retrieved the core and we each shared a piece of the core.

Unfortunately, as we chewed on the pear we started howling because the bristles were sticking to our tongue. To make matters worse in handling the pears we accidentally got slivers on our hands and they were painful and almost impossible to remove.

So the next time we climbed Punchbowl we decided to give the pinee-nees a wide berth and stuck to hiking and sledding on the mountain slope.

SHOOT HIM!!SHOOT HIM!!

When Grandpa Bigdog lived in Honolulu, one of the homes he occupied was on Awaiolimu Street. There were two houses on our lot, the front one which we occupied for a few years and later when Mr. Rodriguez son-in-law got married, he wanted our house. So we moved behind the first house.

Just across the street on the corner of Whiting Street and Awaiolimu Street were a high stonewall and a house occupied by Mr. and Mrs. Ornellas. Mr. Ornellas was a policeman and kind of a mean guy. His son Sonny Ornellas was a good friend of Uncle Wally and they paled around together a lot.

One of the treasures we enjoyed in Honolulu was the mango. And, Mr. Ornellas has a huge mango tree on the Mauka side of his house loaded with nice mangos. The trouble was that Mr. Ornellas did not share his mangos with anyone. We used to sit across the street looking longingly at that huge tree loaded with ripe mangos and try to find ways to get some of that delicious fruit. Even Sonny Ornellas had trouble getting mangos.

One of the most delicious of any fruit is a stolen fruit. (Years later in Campbell, California GBD used to steal cherries and for some reason they were better tasting than store bought cherries). Same thing with mangos!

So one night Uncle Wally and Sonny Ornellas decided that it was time to get to those delicious mangos. So after dark they plotted a course of action. They decided to sneak up Whiting Street to climb the stone wall and make their way to the mango tree without awakening Mr. Ornellas. Well Uncle Wally and Sonny made it up the tree and began to harvest mangos and stuff them in their shirts.

For some reason they made too much noise and out came Mr. Ornellas with his pistol and with Mrs. Ornellas in her nightshirt following him around the tree. Uncle Wally and Sonny kept still and Mr. Ornellas shouted, "Who's there?"

"Nobody" replied Uncle Wally before he realized what he had done.

"SHOOT HIM. SHOOT HIM", cried Mrs. Ornellas and poor Uncle Wally and Sonny figured that they were going to meet their Maker.

Well, soon a crowd of portagees gathered and in the confusion, Uncle Wally and Sonny escaped up Whiting Street and circled around to join the crowd. Mr. Ornellas asked them if they saw anyone.

"No, we did not see anyone," said Uncle Wally and Sonny with their shirts bulging with mangos.

Soon the crowd broke up and Uncle Wally came home with a shirt full of ripe mangos and escaped death. Lucky for Uncle Wally that Mr. Ornellas did not listen to his wife.

SS HUALALAI

When Grandpa Bigdog lived in Honolulu, there were few means of rapid transportation. There was an inter island airplane which flew to Hilo and Maui and the major means for inter island transportation was by ship. There were two ships that plied the waters around Oahu, the SS Hualalai and the SS Waialiali.

The Hualalai traveled from Honolulu to Lahiana, Maui then onto Hilo. The Waialiali traveled to Kauai and we could always note the departure, since the ship blew its whistle around 9:00 pm at night and headed off to Kauai. The Hualalai left around 5:00 pm, stopped in Lahaina and arrived in Hilo in the early morning. These ships were about 325 feet long and were the mainstay of inter island transportation by sea.

When GBD was six years old, Auntie Maria came to Honolulu on a visit and she offered to take me back with her. So one afternoon we went down to near the Aloha Tower where the SS Hualalai was moored. We did not exactly go first class, but rode steerage that is in the very stern of the ship. The ship left about 5 in the afternoon and headed out past Diamond Head on toward Maui. There were a lot of ropes curled on the deck and you could hear the loud noise of the engine as we plowed on into the sunset. Somewhere around nine o'clock the ship reached Lahaina, Maui where passengers and cargo were unloaded and other passengers embarked and then we were off to Hawaii.

The next morning we approached the big island as the ship moved closer to Hilo, the main city in Hawaii. When the ship docked we went to Auntie Maria and Uncle John's house in Hilo. I remember staying there a few days and visited Uncle John and Auntie Bella, then we were off to Kuka-iau Ranch were Uncle Manuel and Auntie Ida lived with their children Abel, Daniel, Bella and Lydia.

Kukaiau Ranch is on the slopes of Mauna Kea, a large volcano and the highest mountain in Hawaii and the ranch is high in the clouds near the top of the mountain. GBD remembers cousin Able showing me his pet pig that he let out of the pen and chased around the yard. Uncle Manuel was a master craftsman and most likely the best saddle maker on the island. Since they had a lot of cattle and horses on the ranch it was important that there were good saddles and bridles and Uncle Manuel's were the best.

One-day cousin Able and GBD rode a horse up the mountainside through some eucalyptus forest when we came upon a wild turkey with a brood of chicks. We got off the horse and chased the chicks until we rounded up 18 chicks. We thought we really had a great find until the mother turkey flew at us, we dropped the chicks and ran for the horse and rode away.

There were many horses on the ranch and GBD had a great time riding horses. One day GBD got on a horse and rode up to the stable. Cousin Daniel, Uncle Manuel's son, decided to play a trick on GBD and turned the saddle backwards on the horse. Needless to say that was hard to ride. After I put up a fuss he returned the saddle to the correct way, then I rode the horse back down the road past Uncle Adolph's house. When GBD turned the horse around the horse took off and ran toward the stable. GBD got scared and threw the bridle away and hung on to the pommel (saddle horn). Auntie Ida was watching out the window of her house and wondered why I was riding so fast, but I couldn't stop the horse. When we reached the gate, the horse suddenly stopped and GBD got down. That was enough horseback riding for one day.

Auntie Ida had a Maytag washing machine on the lower level of the house powered by a gasoline engine. GBD had never seen one before and thought that was unusual. GBD remembers that the exhaust pipe ran under ground and came out near the road.

Another thing that was unusual was the fog. Since Kukaiau Ranch is so high, clouds form around Mauna Kea and this creates a dense fog that sweeps down the mountain and is really strange. It was difficult to see and sometimes the cloud lingered for a long time.

After leaving the ranch, GBD spent some time with Auntie Nora in Honokaa. Uncle Alfred ran a grocery store and we were always so grateful to them because each year at Christmas, Uncle Alfred sent a big box with candy and goodies for us.

One day GBD and cousin Ella had a penny each and Auntie Nora told us not to spend it on candy. Well Ella and I went to the store and bought licorice suckers and began eating them in the back yard. When Auntie Nora called us, we hid the candy under some wood and went into the house. She asked us if we had bought candy and we lied, "No". But since the licorice was black, our faces were all smeared with black candy and that gave us away.

Uncle Manuel and Auntie Ida's home
on Kukaiau Ranch

One day Uncle Ernest Awong took us down to see Auntie Mary at Haina. There is a big sugar mill and we got to see how they crushed cane to make sugar. There were huge crushing wheels that crushed the cane stalks. We also went by the rail cars and pulled cane stalks from the cars and cut off pieces of cane to chew. That is really delicious.

Finally, GBD went back on the SS Hualalai to Honolulu. That was a trip I shall never forget.

KANAKAS EVERYWHERE

When Grandpa was a young boy he lived on the slopes of Punchbowl, an extinct crater in Honolulu. Grandpa and Uncle Paul found a way to make bobsleds from wood and slide down the steep slopes of the volcano. Since the volcano was covered with grass we had to smash the grass down to make a trail down the mountain. Once we established a trail, it was smooth sail and we really flew down the mountain. This was great except.....

There were some hazards in the way of our fun. You see there were guava stumps in the grass and if we hit them we would go flying off the sled. This was not bad except that there were pinene bushes all over the slopes. Pinene bushes are cactus plants full of sharp thorns and if you landed in one of them it would really see stars. Another hazard were the Kanakas.

Above Punchbowl on the slopes of Mt. Tantalus was a Hawaiian settlement. We called them Kanakas, which is a Hawaiian name for Hawaiian men. The Kanakas also were not too friendly to Uncle Paul and Grandpa. Every time we would spend hours making a trail, they would come along and drive us off and take over our trail. One day just after we made a new trail they came along, twelve of them and drove us off. So, Uncle Paul came up with a great idea.

A few days later, Uncle Paul and I took our sled up the mountain and began the slow process of making a new slide trail. It was steep and we really had a good time, but at the end of the trail was a large guava stump hidden in the grass and a huge clump of pinenes at the end of the trail. So Uncle Paul figured that we could slide down and just before we got to the stump, we would roll off the sled into the grass, because if we hit the stump, we would fly into the pinenes and see a lot of stars. This worked so well we had a great time until.....the Kanakas showed up.

About ten of them with a large sled made from two by fours came up dragging the huge sled behind them. They told us to scram or else. Uncle Paul in turn told them that he would give them a push to get started. So the sled loaded with ten kanakas went roaring down the trail all laughing until they hit the guava stump and went flying into the pinenes!

Meanwhile, Uncle Paul and Grandpa ran for our lives to the sound of screams from the cactus thorns as the Kanakas got their just desserts.

THEY FIRED WHO...??

Any one who lived in Campbell, California in the late 30's to 50's knew that this town was a very unique place. This was well documented in a book by Jeanette Watson entitled "CAMPBELL The Orchard City" that is very interesting reading.

One of the interesting things about Campbell was the communications system. Since the town was the center of prune and apricot farming, there was little affluence and not too many people had telephones. So if one needed to know anything it was a simple matter of going to the Campbell Shoe Shop to ask Tony DeMaria for an update. The other means of communication was to just ask anyone on the street.

"Have you seen Bob Hall or Paul Harris?" someone might ask.

"Oh yea, Paul was heading down to Nelson's Trucking on Foote Street about half an hour ago and Bob Hall was heading over to Pete Ragus' house to throw some footballs around," was an appropriate reply. So in this manner one would be able to keep up on what was happening in town.

Enter Joe Furtado a.k.a. **THE KINGFISH.**

The Kingfish was a local legend like Murray Martin, the owner of Murray's Place on Bascome Avenue. He drove the biggest car in town was quite a lady's man and everyone knew the Kingfish.

One of the big employers in Campbell was Drew's Cannery. They canned apricots, peaches, pears, fruit cocktail and in the winter spinach. This was a great place to obtain summer employment for the locals and the high school kids. My first assignment at Drew's was as a pie boy during apricot season. The next year I got a job as an electrician and had pretty good employment.

But the Kingfish was an executive at Drew's and the big talk around town was that if they ever fired the Kingfish, the cannery would shut down. The Kingfish did a lot of socializing and was a regular customer practicing at the bar of Tony Raffanti's Busy Bee restaurant and bar and made sure that people never forgot his important post at the cannery.

Well one day the 'lightning hit the outhouse'. Joe Furtado got fired!!

Word quickly spread around confidants who worked at the cannery and within a few milliseconds reached Tony at the Shoe Shop. **THE KINGFISH GOT FIRED!!**

Near panic arose in town since everyone knew that if the Kingfish ever got fired the cannery would shut down. This could be the end of affluence in Campbell for those who worked there. After the shock and a few aftershocks the town returned to normal, though there was a lot of talk at Tony's and Murray's Bar of this major earthquake that struck Campbell without warning.

Oh, by the way, Joe Furtado, the Kingfish, drove the garbage truck.

TEST DRIVE

When Grandpa Bigdog lived in Hawaii during the depression, we had very little in toys or playthings, so we had to make our own toys or invent games. We could create many hours of fun to pass the time of day without expensive toys.

One of our fun activities was in the area of transportation and here we resorted to a discarded skate to provide a means of locomotion. There were three ways to make use of a discarded skate. The first was to use a single skate and skate on one foot, but this was a problem, since we had to wear a shoe to use a skate and we did not wear shoes in Honolulu. The second way was to split the skate in two and attach the parts to a two by four. Then we made it into a scooter and this was easy to make and fun to ride. The third way was to build a skate car and this is what we preferred.

Uncle Paul was good at building things from wood and he could cut out nice parts from wood scraps. Our friends also made skate cars and we tried to outdo each other to see who could make the most interesting car.

Well one Friday afternoon we found an old skate and that was like finding treasure. So after some discussion between Uncle Paul and GBD, we decided to make a skate car instead of a scooter. First we had to dismantle the skate to get the wheels. Then we looked around for some large spikes that would be used for the axles. Next we looked for some wood, rope for steering and fence nails to hold the axles to the frame.

Uncle Paul cut out the frame that was a board for the seat to which a two by four was nailed so we could attach the rear axle. Then we made a front axle and attached the wheels using the fence nails to hold the wheels in place. Using fence nails, we attached two pieces of rope to the front axle to allow us to steer the skate car.

Well, Uncle Paul decided to really fancy up this skate car. We worked all day Saturday on this project. He decided to build a hood to make it look like a real car. Then GBD got two soup cans and attached them to the front of the hood to look like headlights. We also found two small tuna fish cans and attached them on the back to look like tail lights. Because of these extras, we did not finish the skate car until Sunday afternoon.

Now for the Test Ride!

Sunday afternoon Uncle Paul and GBD dragged the skate car up Boyd Lane to Lusitana Street. This is where the sidewalks were and that would provide a good test road for our new skate car. Uncle Paul sat down in the driver's seat and I pushed him down the sidewalk, past Bush Lane and over to Kuakini Street. When we reached Kuakini Street, Uncle Paul decided to cross over to the other side of Lusitana Street in front of Eddie Medeiros house where the sidewalk was smoother.

On the corner of Holy Ghost Hill and Lusitana Street lived Mrs. Freitas and next to her was Eddie's house. Now it was my turn to drive and Uncle Paul pushed me up the street toward San Antonio Street. Well, we got halfway up the street when a Police Car pulled up and took away our skate car. It seems that Mrs. Freitas had called the police because we made too much noise. That was a short Test Drive.

TOOTHACHE

When Grandpa Bigdog and Uncle Paul lived in Hawaii we were on welfare and had to depend on charity healthcare. One of our problems was getting dental care. Some of our early experiences with dentists were at Palama Settlement. Palama Settlement was on School Street near Kalihi Heights and we would take a streetcar from Awaiolimu Street down to King Street then up Kalihi Street and get off on School Street. (Many times we walked all the way there and back or got a ride from Uncle Martin, who lived nearby). From there we walked over to Palama Settlement and got to see a Doctor or Dentist.

If we had a cavity we would go there and get our teeth filled with a lot of pain since they didn't use anesthetics for drilling or filling. Another place we went for dental care was next to Our Lady of Peace church and one time the dentist slapped Uncle Paul because he was moving around during the drilling from the pain. Grandma Olivia never took us back there.

One of the problems we had was that our fillings would come out leaving a hole in the tooth. While this did not result in an immediate toothache, we faced a bigger hazard....guavas!!

Guavas are delicious fruits that grow wild in the hills and have hard seeds. We were always looking for ripe guavas and would devour them as soon as we found one, but there was a real price to pay. As we chewed the guavas, usually one of the hard seeds would find its way into our open tooth cavity and then the sparks flew. The guavas seed would stick fast in the cavity and then we had a perpetual tooth ache until we could get to the dentist again.

After leaving Hawaii, we moved to Campbell, California and there we encountered the extinguished Dr. Wyland R. Morgan, DDS. He had a dental practice there and was the only dentist in town. Everyone in town owed him money. His office was next to the Southern Pacific Railroad tracks. He did not use novocaine and having to visit him was like a trip to a torture chamber. Most of the Campbell natives were stuck with his professionalism and torture. Kent Clark, whose father owned Clark's Drug Store, finally found a solution and snuck of to Los Gatos for dental care....we couldn't afford that.

GBD recalls one memorable afternoon after school. It appears that two of my molars, upper and lower had cavities. Well, the torture started as he drilled into my lower jaw with smoke pouring out of my mouth and a lot of pain. Then he found that he needed to place a paste over the nerve before filling the tooth. This involved shoving a piece of paste down into the cavity and nearly pushed me onto the floor. As I wallowed in pain he set a time clock for 90 seconds to see if the pain would subside. If so, he could then fill the tooth. Well, the pain receded and he filled the tooth. Next was the upper molar and GBD went through t he roof as he pushed paste into the upper cavity. By the time I left the torture chamber, I was completely exhausted.

Most of our family had the privilege of accessing dental care from Dr. Morgan. His office waiting room was full of old National Geographic Magazines. Reading these magazines was usually interrupted by shouts of pain from the resident victim sitting in his infamous chair.

After Dr. Morgan retired, his chair was placed in the Campbell Museum and GBD had the pleasure of seeing the chair on a visit to Campbell a few years ago. We should take good care of our teeth so that we don't have to endure a visit to Dr. Morgan's famous chair.

WORD PROBLEMS

One of the most powerful weapons in existence is the word. A word or two can cause embarrassment, humiliation, loss of relationships or disruption of meetings. One of my encounters with word power occurred when I was student teaching at Los Gatos High School. I was teaching Advanced Algebra and I started student teaching in the middle of a semester when the topic was Word Problems. You know how those go. A can run 3 times faster than B and C can only run ½ as fast as B. How fast can D run? Well, I was working my way through San Jose State as a movie projectionist and worked till midnight every day. On this occasion I did not do all the homework problems and decided to wing it. To make matters worse I had an antagonist in Dr. Herman Jameson, who for some reason did not like me since he thought I was Italian, and on this day came to observe my teaching.

"Mr. Miranda, could you work number 14?" a young lady who sat in the first row asked. So I began to work the problem on the board and found the answer to be 54. Then I turned to the answer page and said: "The answer is 36". So I reworked the problem again and got the same answer. At that point Dr. Jameson shouted from the back of the room:

"The answer book is wrong and if you had done your homework you would have found the mistake."

In another instance we had a Director of Research, Dr. W. Gale Cutler who was a real stickler for spelling and I got caught red handed by him once much to my embarrassment. I had written a letter to a Director at Bosch-Siemens and misspelled Dr. Wenning's name. The next morning I found Gale standing at my office door with a copy of my letter. What an embarrassment!

One of the practices in large corporations is to have a number of outside directors to provide counsel and broaden the awareness of other industries for the Board Chairman. For example, John Platts was Whirlpool's Chairman and he was elected to the board of Shell, who in turn chose a director from Shell. One of the directors that Whirlpool selected was the Vice-President of Pepsi, Vic Bonomo. He was a rising star at Pepsi, somewhat arrogant and soon after paid a visit to Whirlpool to visit the campus and be hosted by the Whirlpool Officers.

A lot of preparation faced the campus staff. For example all refrigerators were stripped of Coke, and competitive products. The cafeteria was meticulously cleansed and all was ready to host this important guest.

On the big day Vic was welcomed by the Whirlpool Chairman and Officers and all were prepared for a profitable day exploring Whirlpool until one word spoiled the whole day. The Chairman greeted and sang the praises of Vic to all present then put down the first slide on the VU Graph. Vic leaped to his feet and stormed out of the room and told his guests he was ready to leave and was never so insulted. What word drove him out?
On the agenda there appeared this one item,

3:00 p.m. ——————COKE BREAK—————-Conference Room

*****

Part II

SOCIO-POLITICAL ISSUES

THE BOZONE LAYER

One of the most interesting features of our earth is the ozone layer. This is a belt of ozone about 300 miles above the earth that if not present would make the earth unsuitable for life as we know it! Ozone is prepared by the interaction of intense ultraviolet radiation on oxygen that splits the oxygen molecule to an activated oxygen atom which reacts with oxygen. The process is a steady state system where the amount of ozone produced each day is equal to the amount of ozone consumed. Thus, the ozone layer prevents harmful radiation from striking the earth.

Some of the harmful effects of ozone include the degradation or rubber and certain plastics, the formation of smog when ozone reacts with hydrocarbons in the atmosphere that causes respiratory problems in humans and animals.

The presence of the ozone depletion problem is a boon for those who prosper in the fear business. Politicians require the use of fear to control the masses and can use situations like the ozone depletion problem to scare people into enacting harmful legislation to control quixotic adventures to control this or that in our environment. Other examples include labeling carbon dioxide as a pollutant and developing wasteful legislation and huge losses to our treasure to try to stamp out excess carbon dioxide, ignoring the fact that vegetation and the ocean are enormous sinks for absorbing this gas.

What is more unfortunate is that children are taught this misinformation and soon bring this knowledge to parents who in many cases tend to side with mostly junk science proposals to control natural phenomenon. To further compound the folly, the main stream media help spread the lies that have a large impact on an ignorant population. For example, when the Global Warming crisis emerged, politicians like Al Gore led the charge and became quite rich spewing fear among the population and launching a Green Environment that has hurt our economy and enriched the purveyors of Global Warming..

Meanwhile, the media helped when they reported that 2,200 **Concerned scientists** signed a petition to control carbon dioxide, while 19,000 **Renegade scientists** (including this author) signed a petition declaring Global Warming a HOAX.

So much for an unbiased media!

Gary Larson a famous cartoonist depicted the problem very precisely when he drew a cartoon titled the Bozone Layer. That is a layer of Bozos about 300 feet above Environmentalists that prevents common sense from emerging to deflate lunatic legislation that is costly and needless and destructive.

BUTTER AND ROLLS

When I worked at Whirlpool our management encouraged us to work in the community to promote civic and cultural activities. One day Dr. Gale Cutler, Research Director at the R&E Center asked me to attend a meeting of the Benton Harbor Chamber of Commerce's Executive Lecture Series.

Living in Granger I had little contact with many of the local people. During this meeting they explained the mission of the Executive Lecture Series which was select topics and leading lecturers who could present an afternoon seminar on selected topics of interest to the Benton Harbor/St. Joseph area. At the end of the meeting the Chairman announced that he was resigning and suggested that I become the Chairman, a post that I held for ten years.

At that time there was a lot of interest in motivational behavior, psychological implications in the business community and various management topics. One of our famous speakers was Herb Cohen who was a recognized expert in negotiations. In fact he gave me an autographed copy of his book, "YOU CAN NEGOTIATE ANYTHING". [More about him in another story]

A very famous Professor of Psychology at USC was available to conduct a seminar for us so we invited him and sent notices to the business community about the upcoming seminar. [These seminars were well attended and quite successful]

So on the appointed day I met the Professor at the Benton Harbor airport and drove him to the luncheon. He was dressed in a beautiful black linen suit that with a bow tie would look like an expensive tuxedo. I commented to him about his suit and he told us an interesting tale.

He said that he could board a plane in Los Angeles and fly to Washington, DC and there would not be a wrinkle in the suit and that was the reason he chose this type of apparel. This Professor had been enlisted to debrief Vietnam POW's on their release and was well recognized as an expert in this area.

In the course of time he was invited to speak at a Senate luncheon. So he hopped a plane in LA and flew to DC arriving near noon. As he entered the Senate Dining Room he was surprised that no one was there to greet him, so he stood around assuming that he would eventually be recognized.

Finally, Ted Kennedy raised his hand and beckoned him to his table. Satisfied that he had been recognized he strolled over to Ted's table.

"Can we have some more rolls and butter?" asked Senator Kennedy.

"I am the luncheon speaker" replied the Professor.

During the Professors speech he glanced over at Ted who was cowering at his table anticipating the Professor bringing up the goof, but he decided not to.

Lucky for Ted, who has now been sober for more than two weeks.

COMDOMS

Our current political correct climate has been a disaster for truth and personal freedom. Citizens are now afraid to speak the truth without fear of career ending comments or words that may cause one to be ostracized or denied acceptance in a group. For those who have lived long enough to have witnessed the demise of our once great country, we must look back to 1910 when a group of evil bankers and politicians crafted the Federal Reserve System that has given us perpetual wars, the income tax and creeping loss of freedom and fiscal sanity

The real culprit is the voter who was willing to give up pieces of freedom in exchange for security; financial or personal. Voters began electing politicians who gave us legislation that produced the Civil Rights movement and government support of out of wedlock parenting destroying the family as we knew it. This created a society that became more dependent on government handouts and the fulfillment of Professor Tyler's prophesy *"that a democracy cannot last more than two hundred years because voters will learn to vote largess out of the treasury"*.

For those who can tolerate truth, let me provide a few examples of the issue. Benton Harbor in the early fifties, was the jewel of southwestern Michigan. There were beautiful homes, parks and the place to live since so many of Whirlpool's middle and upper management lived in the Fairplain section of town. St. Joseph, a Twin City, was also a beautiful city. Meanwhile, Detroit was another great city bustling with manufacturing plants, beautiful homes and apartment buildings as was Flint, Michigan.

Today those cities are a disaster. The last time I visited Detroit, I gave a lecture at the University of Detroit and on my way to the airport, I was driven down Livernois Avenue. It looked like the German tanks just left an hour ago. Total disaster!!

I was discussing this with a friend the other evening and he pointed out that there is a Common Denominator that is the root cause of the problem. These cities have been taken over by an influx of blacks and political correctness requires that we have black leaders, many who are incompetent, that have destroyed these cities. PC does not allow the correct term to describe these people, so my friend refers to them as **COMMON DENOMINATORS.** A perfect term Steve, so let us now call them:

COMDOMS!

EINSTEIN'S EQUATION

Dr. Albert Einstein was one of the world's greatest Physicists and Theoretical Scientist! His greatest contributions are well known to many in the scientific and lay world as he developed theories about photoelectric effects, gravity and the relationship between mass and energy. This last discovery led to the production of the atomic bomb and later to major developments in the field of Nuclear Energy.

H. Hertz first noted the photoelectric effect. Later Einstein developed his photoelectric theory by explaining the effect of light striking alkali metals and ejecting electrons. Einstein's Photoelectric Theory can be expressed by this equation:

$$Hf = w_0 + \tfrac{1}{2} mv^2$$

Where h=Planck's constant 6.62×10^{-27} ergxsec; f = frequency, $w_0 =$ work function m = mass and v=velocity.

Later Einstein turned his attention to gravity and the relationship of mass to energy. He showed that gravity can bend a light wave and his theory was confirmed in an experiment during a total eclipse of the sun. This brought him considerable fame.

Meanwhile, Max Planck showed that energy and light could be related by a simple equation:

$$E = hv$$

Where energy is related to the frequency of light (v) in cycles per second and h is Planck's constant. Einstein later showed that Energy is related to mass by his now famous equation:

$$E = mc^2$$

Where Energy is equal to the mass in grams and the speed of light 3×10^{10} meters/second squared.

After Einstein died historians sought access to his many notes and papers scattered all over his desk at Princeton University. They were startled to discover that prior to his death he had become very interested in the phenomenon of Global Warming and was working on a mathematical relationship to describe the phenomenon in the form of an equation. His hand written notes showed that he was successful in this effort, but due to his illness he never published his work. Now for the first time we have a mathematical solution to the problem as described in the new Einstein equation:

$$G_w = gB/\pi$$

Where G_w = Global Warming Hoax
   g = The Gore constant that is useless and equal to zero
   B = BS a Natural product found in Bull Pens (and also in the congress)
   π = A number that goes on forever.

Thanks Albert.

FO

In recent years Americans have seen the quality of national leadership drop into the tank. It seems that we cannot develop leaders who follow the constitution, but accept selected people to lead us. Much of this can be blamed on the Federal Reserve Act in 1913 where congress abdicated its power to regulate money to world bankers. In the United States the Federal Reserve, which is neither Federal nor has any reserves have taken over and we have seen bad business cycles and perpetual wars to sustain their money regulating powers.

One of the key groups is the Bilderberg Group that meets in secret each year to set the agenda and when timely, select the candidates for President. Many people were amazed when an unknown peanut farmer suddenly broke onto the stage and was hailed as a great leader. Jimmy Carter made a march across Georgia to campaign for President. His picture appeared on Time Magazine and he was eventually elected President.

The media hailed this genius as a nuclear engineer who understood nuclear power. He certainly did since one of his major accomplishments was to shut down a Breeder Reaction project that would have converted spent nuclear fuel to usable fuel. Other successes followed. The interest rates soared to 21% and unemployment rose as well as taxes.

Jimmy has a great talent for indecision!

When the Iranians stormed our embassy and took hostages, the first thing he wanted was a book on Islam so he could better understand the problem (See Free the Hostages). While he was learning he hid in the Rose Garden and blamed the American people for malaise.

When the Carters settled in the White House they decided to place Amy in a public school. Soon the media began referring to the fact that Amy was attending a *ghetto* school.

One of my tasks at Whirlpool was to cover the impact of Government Regulations on our business climate related to coatings and polymers. As a result I used to visit Washington to attend meetings of the Association of Home Appliance Manufacturers, AHAM. Their headquarters was next to the *ghetto* school that Amy attended. I could see the school and school yard from the conference room where we met. There were photographers in the play yard taking pictures. This was a big deal for the drive-by media. It was definitely not a ghetto school.

Well one night at dinner Jimmy asked Amy a question.

"Amy what is 2+2?"

Amy promptly replied: FO

The next day they placed Amy into a private school.
The drive-by media responded with Enthusiastic Silence!

FREE THE HOSTAGES

When I worked at Whirlpool our management encouraged us to work in the community to promote civic and cultural activities. One day Dr. Gale Cutler, Research Director at the R&E Center asked me to attend a meeting of the Benton Harbor Chamber of Commerce's Executive Lecture Series.

During this meeting they explained the mission of the Executive Lecture Series which was select topics and leading lecturers who could present an afternoon seminar on selected topics of interest to the Benton Harbor/St. Joseph area. At the end of the meeting the Chairman announced that he was resigning and suggested that I become the Chairman, a post that I held for ten years.

At that time there was a lot of interest in motivational behavior, psychological implications in the business community and various management topics. One of our famous speakers was Herb Cohen who was a recognized expert in negotiations. In fact he gave me an autographed copy of his book, "YOU CAN NEGOTIATE ANYTHING".

Our committee agreed to have Herb present a seminar and it was well attended. Herb is a dynamic speaker and told an interesting story about his first job where he had an interesting encounter with the Japanese. Herb had pressed for an assignment on negotiations with a Japanese firm where he could demonstrate his skills as a negotiator. So Herb arrived in Japan for a 4 day meeting where he was supposed to negotiate a favorable agreement with the Japanese.

Instead of getting down to business as Herb had planned, his adversaries suggested that he join them in a visit of some famous tourist sites. The next day they again engaged him in more visits and wining and dining.

Finally on the last day late in the afternoon the Japanese sat down to negotiate a deal and with little time to argue so he 'gave away the store'. His visit was a total disaster.

During the Carter Administration, Iranians stormed the U. S. Embassy in Tehran and took hostages. The first thing the Carter Nobel Laureates in the White House did was to send for Herb Cohen. They presented the problem to him and asked him how he could negotiate the release of the hostages. Herb presented his solution:

- Monday cut off medical supplies to Iran.
- Tuesday cut of all food supplies.
- Wednesday freeze all assets.
- Thursday begin bombing Iran.
- Friday the hostages come home.

The Nobel Laureates in the Carter Administration told Herb that they couldn't do that.

So Herb told them that in such a case the hostages would not come home until January 21, fifteen months later.

And so it was that Carter rejected Herb's solution and it took the election of Ronald Reagan to free the hostages 15 months later.

OLD SETTLERS DAY

When I moved to Campbell, California in 1942, I found a completely different culture from that in Hawaii. Honolulu is a big city stretching for many miles from near Pearl Harbor to Diamond Head and Waikiki Beach. Campbell on the other hand was a very small town along the Southern Pacific Railroad tracks and featured a fruit cannery, dehydrator and a lumberyard. Most of the commercial part was along Campbell Avenue including Clark's Drug Store, Dr. Morgan's Dental Office, the Post Office, two barbershops, Campbell Shoe Hospital (Tony DeMaria's Shoe Shop the communication center of Campbell) a hardware store, Garcia's Plumbing Shop and Nelson's Feed and Grain. Along Foote Street was Nelson Trucking who was a big hauler of fruit and freight.

The most exciting thing that happened in town was when the switch engine came to Drew's Cannery to drop off boxcars full of empty cans and to carry away canned fruit. Then of course there was the passenger train returning from San Francisco via Los Gatos about 7:30 each night.

For entertainment there was the Campbell Theater and I served there for a few years as projectionist working for $4.00 a night. Other forms of entertainment involved watching Jack Vitale drive his 1938 Dodge onto the railroad tracks or visiting Tony DeMaria at the shoe shop to find out what was going on in town. For those of the proper age there was the Busy Bee Bar owned by Tony Raffanti. Anyone who was anyone, such as the Kingfish, Murray Martin and other notables were well known at Tony's.

A major event in Campbell was Old Settler's Day, February 22, also Washington's Birthday. This was a big holiday and it honored the Old Settlers who has settled the town many years ago. The highlight was a big parade through town with many businesses represented, the High School Band, Kiwanis Club and other who made floats for the parade.

During World War II there was a big shortage of many things including rubber goods and this posed a problem for the folks who made floats for the parade. Since toy balloons were almost impossible to obtain during the war the floats would be without balloons....except for those with imagination and creativity.

So here is the big parade! The floats go by: Nelson Grain a big flat bed with bales of hay, feed sacks, then other floats and the one that promoted the most laughter was Garcia Plumbing. On the flatbed truck they had placed a few toilets, a bathtub and some of the plumbers sitting on the toilet seats. These creative guys had balloons on their float and embarrassed looks on the plumber's faces as the crowd tried to be polite. It seems that they did manage to get some balloons, but probably from Clark's Drug Store, since the balloons were all elongated and meant for other purposes.

Old Settler's Day is a big event in Campbell.

$$\varphi\, \tau\, \alpha$$

When Grandpa Bigdog was in the Army Chemical Corps, he was stationed at the Army Chemical Center in Edgewood, Maryland. This was a high security post that manufactured nerve gas. There were also a large chemical laboratory and a biological laboratory for studying the physiological effects of nerve gas. I worked on the latter and also studied the physiology of nerve gas antidotes. This post consisted of a Military Police Detachment and Detachment 3 that was the home of Scientific Professional Personnel (SPP's) that were chemists, engineers and scientists. Our detachment commander was Captain Kmiotek and the administrative head was Staff Sergeant Giannini who really ran the detachment. There were a number of chemists who had graduated from Notre Dame University and they sang the praises of the chemistry department. After leaving the Army I attended Notre Dame and met Lew Taft who was a graduate student and who later was drafted and sent to the ACC.

In the lobby just outside the Captain's office there was a large two-sided bulletin board where the orders of the day were posted and certain assignments, like KP or personnel's transfer orders would appear every day. For example a note would be posted that read:

The following men will pull targets tomorrow:
T2 THOMAS MIRANDA
PFC CLIFFORD POLLARD
T2 DONALD STOFFEY

A few milliseconds after the posting, the following would appear somewhere on the note

The following men will pull targets tomorrow:
T2 THOMAS MIRANDA
PFC CLIFFORD POLLARD
T2 DONALD STOFFEY   φτα

φ τ α

Phi Tau Alpha had a very derogatory connotation and all of the SPP's learned the meaning of this Greek term on the first day we landed in Detachment 3. Phi Tau Alpha was translated "F*** The Army" as most of us couldn't wait to get out. We even had stickers made with these words that I had pasted on the dashboard of my car. One day I was driving to Detachment 3 when I spotted an MP thumbing a ride. When he saw that he asked me what it meant and I told him it was a Greek word meaning "For The Army". He thought that was great, since he was regular army.

In Captain Kmiotek's office there was a picture of President Eisenhower signing a bill. One night the CQ took the picture apart and just under the President's pen he wrote φτα and restored the picture to its rightful place behind the Captain's chair. That remained for a long time until after the annual picnic at the Bush River.

Our post commander was General Cressey who was later transferred to the Pentagon and replaced with a recently promoted Colonel, General Burns. Being recently promoted General Burns had to make a show of his authority and began changing rules that were more to the liking of the SPP's under General Cressey.

It was almost impossible to escape those three letters, which were written all over the post bulletin boards, letters and anything related to army events. Speaking of events, we had an annual picnic at the Bush River with swimming, beer, hot dogs and the big event where General Burns would make his appearance to visit the troops. Cosmo the cook had baked a large sheet cake and it was beautifully decorated:

φ τ α

ACC PICNIC

FOURTH OF JULY

After an afternoon of fun and games the time for dessert was at hand and Cosmo the Cook asked General Burns if he would like to cut the first slice and the General agreed.

The General admired the cake and finally asked Beetle Bailey (Robert Bailey worked in the General's office and was also an SPP):

"What is that PTA at the top of the cake?"
Beetle responded, "Why that is Greek, Sir."
"Phi Tau Alpha, means: "For The Army"
"Great" said General Burns, "I like that"

The General was completely taken in and went around saying φτα to anyone who would listen. Well shortly after that the lightning hit the outhouse! Somehow General Burns learned the real meaning of these Greek letters and things began to happen. The General ordered Courts Martial for anyone affixing this endearing note to any bulletin board or anywhere else. So that ended the fun though thinking in Greek went on among the troops.

I wonder if General Burns ever saw the photo of President Eisenhower in Captain Kmiotek's office?

SEAT BELTS

When air travel began people were required to use seat belts on take-off and landings as a measure of safety. This makes good sense because in the early days, aircraft did not fly at high altitudes and most of the travel was through weather. Meanwhile, automobile drivers and passengers did not use seat belts and with government rules and pressure from unaccountable pressure groups we found that seat belts are now required and non use may result in some kind of punishment.

The idea that we need laws to compel us to use such a common sense solution is somewhat baffling, but many people ignore the law and more importantly, their common sense and suffer the consequences.

When I joined Whirlpool in 1968, Carol and I decided against moving to Benton Harbor or St. Joseph and decided to remain in Granger. This required me to drive about 40 miles one way each day to work in Benton Harbor. The worst part of the drive was driving up US 31 a two lane highway with many opportunities for an accident. During my early years I did not use a seat belt.

I worked at the Elisha Gray II Research and Engineering Center. We had a number of very talented scientists and engineers there and it was a great place to work. One of the most impressive men there was Ed Peterson, a physicist. In my opinion I felt that Ed was one of the sharpest knives in the drawer. He had a uncanny ability to see through complex problems and solve them and also had a good memories of past mistakes that we had made on product development and would be able so short circuit wasteful projects that had proved failures at Whirlpool or other companies. Ed was also creative in that he and Dr. John Blatchford developed conductive porcelain that could be used to produce a range free of conventional burners. He was also an expert on static electricity. Static electricity is important in vacuum cleaners and clothes drying and Ed had a laboratory dedicated to the measurement of static high voltages.

My office faced the parking lot and every day at noon I used to notice that Ed would run out to his old Volkswagon bus and the first thing he did was to fasten his seat belt.

I then reasoned that if Ed, smart as he is, would use a seat belt, perhaps I should start using a seat belt. That Friday evening I used my seat belt. The following week I was driving through Berrien Springs. I became involved in a head-on accident that should have thrown me out of the car had I not been wearing my seat belt.

I shall always be grateful to Ed for his good common sense example.

Thanks Ed.

STRINGS

Back in the sixties there was a lot of free government money due to President Johnson's Great Society extravaganza. This led to many non government organizations being funded to study problems that the Great Society needed to resolve. But there was a problem, the money had a long string attached.

During that period, South Bend had a Republican mayor, Lloyd Allen, who had accepted a large hand out to improve the city, the big dollars rolled in and Michigan Avenue was stripped of its businesses to make way for a downtown mall paid for by Federal Funds. There were many big stores in South Bend like Sears, Penneys, Robertson's, a family owned business as was Wymans. In addition there were many theaters. On Michigan Avenue there were The Palace, now the Morris Civic Center, The Granada, The State and The Avon. Also on Colfax Avenue was the Colfax Theater. When I was attending Notre Dame I worked as a relief projectionist and stage hand at all of these theaters. And that was good supplemental income.

On any given day the downtown was bustling with shoppers, parking was always a problem and the city resorted to building parking garages. One garage was built on Wayne Street and the first floor was below grade level causing some embarrassment to the city engineer.

Meanwhile, as South Bend began to tear up Michigan Avenue and displacing over forty businesses, those businesses moved to Mishawaka and that city has grown by leaps and bounds. South Bend soon found itself saddled with forced bussing, dumbing down of the schools and numerous Civil Rights obligations. John Adams High School, a jewel in the crown of Indiana High Schools fell from its high academic perch as well as other high schools in the system. The cost of bussing was enormous and no improvement in educational test scores was demonstrated. Those strings did indeed stretch a long way to D.C.

The Studebaker Corporation went bankrupt and left a large area of auto building facilities empty. The Studebaker Foundry was a jewel in the manufacturing business so Cummins decided to buy the facility to build engine blocks. Cummins is a well managed company that makes diesel engines of high quality. After a short stay in South Bend, Cummins pulled out citing poor profit as a motive for leaving. The truth was that affirmative action and its consequences made their managing style inoperable in South Bend.

Allen was followed by Roger Parent a democratic mayor who never earned a dollar from a business enterprise only from government funds. Parent decided to build a baseball stadium but the people were opposed and voted against the measure. Only 34% of the voters favored the effort and Parent was elated that so many were in favor. So they built the Coveleski Stadium.

Not to be outdone Mayor Kernan another democrat in collusion with the hierarchy at Notre Dame conspired to bring the College Football Hall of Fame (Shame?) to South Bend. Mayor Kernan publically announced that not penny of tax money would go to support this waste. The only hero in this episode was Jim Czerniak who fought a losing battle with financial facts and the bad history of the Hall of Fame in Ohio. Now South Bend loses about a million dollars a year and is saddled with a 20 year bond payment.

So between government money with long strings attached and a single party system of government South Bend is heading for a scrap yard of poorly run cities.

"When small men begin to cast large shadows, it is a sure sign that the sun is setting"

REMEMBERING PEARL HARBOR

As in all major historical events, people who witness these events have emotional recollections on their anniversaries. The bombing of Pearl Harbor is an historical event firmly imbedded in my memory.

My family lived in Hawaii having come to the islands from Norway and the Madera Islands by sailing ship and settled on sugar plantations on the big island, Hawaii. My two brothers and a sister were born in Hawaii and my younger sister and I were born on Oahu, and were living in Honolulu at the time of the attack.

Prior to the attack the islanders were aware that a war with Japan was inevitable and were preparing for such an event. In fact, there were two black out exercises carried out by the military in the summer of 1941. It was quite a scary event to see the whole city in darkness.

Our family was on welfare since my father had died when I was in the fourth grade and my oldest brother Wallance had just gotten a job at Pearl Harbor as a machinist and worked the night shift on December 6, 1941.

There were many military bases on Oahu as well as two naval bases, Pearl Harbor and Kaneohe Naval Base. We used to watch the big PBY Catalina flying boats flying back to Pearl Harbor at five o'clock in the evening. These large airplanes would fan out each morning at 5 a.m. and return at 5 p.m. Their mission was to scout for enemy ships that might attack the islands.

What was so interesting about this is that on December 7, 1941, the Catalina flying boats did not go out that morning. President Roosevelt ordered General Walter Short to fly only to the southwest. (The Japanese fleet was located in the northwest and had the Catalinas gone out as usual, they would have found the Japanese fleet)

My older brother Paul and I used to love watching navy ships come in to Pearl Harbor. Usually, when the fleet came in the aircraft carriers would stand off Waikiki Beach and that was a sight to behold. I can remember seeing the USS Lexington and USS Yorktown sitting off shore.

On December 6, my brother Paul and I were cranking traps for a skeet club near the Kaneohe Naval Base. A group of Honolulu businessmen had a skeet club near Kapoho Point and for cranking traps were paid $2.50, big money for us since bread was only four cents a loaf. When we finished work, the businessmen took us around the island and dropped us off in Kaimuki. We then took a bus home near Punchbowl, an extinct crater in the center of Honolulu.

The next morning I went to the 7 a.m. mass and got home about 7:40. There was a small park just off Lusitana Street where kids would gather and as I was walking across the park I heard a loud whistle of a shell flying overhead that exploded on the slopes of Punchbowl. Soon several more shells came flying overhead and we kids decided that the military were having maneuvers.

So we looked over at Pearl Harbor and saw a lot of airplanes diving down and huge clouds of black smoke rising. We could see planes diving down then turning up after dropping bombs or torpedoes. Some planes crashed. We watched this from about 8 a.m. on.

As we were standing there we heard fighter planes above with machine guns blazing. All of a sudden a Japanese plane came right over us, about 100 feet in the air. We could see the rising sun on the wing tips and a big sun on the tail. The Japanese pilot was working the control stick for all he was worth; as he was being chased by two P40 fighters with their machine guns blazing. We watched this until they disappeared from view.

After a while, my brother Paul found me in the park and told me there was a war going on. We ran home.

About 10:00 a.m. my brother Paul and sisters Eva, Lorraine and I were standing out on Lusitana Street when we heard a screaming shell coming. We dived behind a stone wall as the shell exploded spraying the wall with hot shrapnel. Paul picked up a piece and it burnt his hand. My sister Eva still has that piece of shrapnel.

My oldest brother Wallance had worked the night shift at Pearl Harbor and was ordered to return to work. On the way in their car was strafed by Japanese planes. When he got to work, he assisted in removing bodies from the USS Oklahoma and taking them to the machine shops. After a few hours he was sent home.

After that we really got worried. The food stores were closed and martial law was declared. The price of a loaf of bread soared from 4 cents to 9 cents a loaf. Anyone caught looting would be shot. At night there was a complete blackout. It was strange to look out at night and not see a single light burning. Rumors that the Japanese had landed spread around the neighborhood. A Japanese pilot crashed on Mt. Tantalus near our home and we saw the pilot being taken away by the military.

One island, Nihau, was captured by the Japanese. The pilot got lost and landed there. He rounded up the villagers and took over the island. After a while he got into an argument with a Hawaiian man. The Japanese pilot shot the man in the abdomen. This angered the Hawaiian who picked up the Japanese pilot and smashed him to the ground killing the pilot. The Hawaiian then got into a boat and rowed to Kauai for help.

Hawaii was placed under martial law. We were all given identification cards, tetanus shots and were required to carry a gas mask with us at all times. Schools reopened, but the high school I attended, Saint Louis College was taken over as a military hospital and the school moved into the McKinley School in Honolulu where I finished my freshman year.

Since we were on welfare and there was a lot of uncertainty about a Japanese invasion, the Red Cross arranged for our family to move to California to live with my grandfather Manuel Miranda in Campbell. So in September, 1942 we boarded the USS Mt. Vernon, a troop ship and sailed off to California. Our brother Wallance who worked at Pearl Harbor remained behind and supported the family.

My brother Paul enlisted in the Navy and survived the sinking of the USS Hoel, DD533 off Samar, my sister Eva joined the Women's Army Corps and I eventually served in the Chemical Corps.

A SIMPLE SOLUTION

One of the most interesting aspects of human behavior is the abhorrence of simple solutions to complex problems! This is true in so many aspects of our daily lives, but an aspect prominent in the political arena.

Here is a list of simple solutions to complex problems that would make this country in particular and the world in general a better place to live:

PROBLEM	SIMPLE SOLUTION
Bad Economy	Lower Taxes and spending; Eliminate Federal Reserve and IRS
Country Bankrupt	Cut all Foreign Aid Eliminate UN
Drugs	Kill all drug users [Singapore does this and has no drug problem]
Illegal Immigration	Close Borders; Shoot Violators
Incompetent Congress	Enforce Constitution; One term only
Morality	Return to God as a nation

What is so ridiculous is that we have the answer to all of these concerns and a solution staring us in the face, but we refuse to act. Imagine being locked up in a dungeon and the key to the lock is in the door, but one refuses to turn the key to freedom. Sounds ridiculous, but it is so true.

Jesus gave us a simple commandment: "*LOVE GOD, LOVE NEIGHBOR*". And what a simple solution to our world problems!!

More significant is the command given in II Chronicles 7:14 that reads: *"If my people, who are called by my name, will humble themselves and pray and seek my face and turn from their wicked ways, then will I hear them from heaven and will forgive their sin and will heal their land"*

Now how much simpler can this get and will the people of this country wake up, turn the key and rush to FREEDOM. And, why is this message not preached everyday in our churches and among Christians to bring this great healing about?

SLUMBER

The Catholic Church has just awakened from their slumber to discover that the Obama Administration has set its secular sights on the Church forcing them to discard their rejection of abortion and birth control. In response, the Bishop had a letter read after Sunday masses alerting Catholics to this outrage.

Surprise! Surprise! The trap was sprung during the 2008 Election!

Where was the Catholic Hierarchy in the 2008 Presidential campaign? Catholics did not hear anything like the Bishop's letter during that campaign even though the Catholic Church knew of this monster and his pro abortion stance and evil.

Meanwhile, the Church responds with enthusiastic silence to the likes of Nancy Pelosi, Joe Biden and other important Catholics who are still allowed to receive the sacraments with impunity. Where is the condemnation of these fake Catholics?

Remember, when Notre Dame University invited Mario the Pius (Governor Cuomo) to speak at Stepan Center? He declared that Capital Punishment was murder, but abortion was Choice. The entire audience leaped to their feet applauding this outrage. Now the Church looks away as Governor Cuomo, the current New York Governor approves gay marriage.

This country was made great by our founders and the preachers who shouted decency and morality from their pulpits and less about the second collection. Will the Catholic Hierarchy have the courage to drive this man from office?

It may be too late now!

SUPPLY AND DEMAND

One of the very important functions of the Quartermaster Corps in any military function is to provide the necessary materials and supplies for an army such as food, clothing, shelter and other needs. This is one of the most critical operations for a successful military campaign and any failure along the line can spell defeat or victory in a campaign.

For example, during the Korean War, the North Koreans were pushing American and South Korean forces back down the Korean Peninsula. General MacArthur was the commander and decided upon retreating in the face of the onslaught. As the North Koreans advanced so did their supply line. Then General MacArthur launched a sweeping attack far behind the enemy lines at Inchon and then drove the North Koreans all the way back to the Yalu River. But winter had set in and the troops were still in their summer uniforms and were faced with a new enemy; **winter**. This is where the Quartermaster Corps had to rush in winter clothing to prevent a disaster, illustrating the importance of the supply and demand issue.

When I was in the Army Chemical Corps, I was stationed at the Army Chemical Center in Edgewood, Maryland where Lew Taft also served. There I met Dr. Theodor Wagner-Jauregg who had been an officer in the German Sixth Army at Stalingrad in 1943. [He was the son of Leopold Wagner-Jauregg, a Nobel Laureate in Medicine.] After WWII he was given the option to come to the United States and took a position at Edgewood Arsenal. There is a chemical reaction named after him involving the condensation of maleic anhydride with unsaturated aromatics like stilbene and similar to the familiar Diels-Alder reaction of dienes and dienophiles

We used to have Friday afternoon seminars at the Army Chemical Center and one day I attended one delivered by Dr. T. Wagner-Jauregg. He told us about his experience with the Sixth Army in Stalingrad at the end of

1942. The German army was under the command of General Friedrich Paulus (who was later made Field Marshal by Hitler) and they had captured Stalingrad but were surrounded by Russian troops. Supplies were running low and periodically a supply plane could break through and replenish the troops. This was an important role for the Quartermaster Corps back in Berlin.

General Paulus devised a plan to defeat the Russians. He decided to fly out the wounded, then retreat south from Stalingrad to where the Volga River was frozen, cross the river then attack the Russians from the west, then proceed down to the Black Sea and the oil resources there. So the Germans began to fly out the wounded on aircraft that were available and Dr. Wagner-Jauregg was fortunate enough to get out in this manner.

Just as General Paulus was about to carry out his plan he received a telegram from Adolph Hitler, "**STAND AND DIE**". So the Germans were defeated. But lucky for the Germans, one plane finally did make it through the blockade. **The Quartermaster Corps did their job!** The soldiers rushed out to the plane only to discover that it was a planeload of condoms.

Just what they needed!

TELEGRAM

It seems that everywhere you go today you see someone with a cell phone glued to their ear, whether driving, shopping on even in a theater. With the communication system we now have it is virtually impossible to retain your privacy. Back in the old days, the thirties and forties, there were no rapid means of communication and the best way to reach anyone quickly was to send a telegram.

The telegram was an important tool for transmitting urgent news that demanded immediate attention! For example, when my Grandfather died in Ookala, Hawaii in the thirties, I remember Uncle Arthur sent my mother a telegram with the sad news.

It was also very common in rail stations and hotel lobbies to hear a telegraph messenger calling out someone's name, "Telegram for Mr. Brown". In the public arena, this also carried an air of importance to certain egotists to hear their name shouted in a crowded room.

My research professor at Notre Dame was Dr. G. Frank D'Alelio a world famous polymer pioneer. He was an unusual man who had only friends and enemies, nothing in between. He had been a Director of Research for General Electric and well known in the industry. He also had a high vapor pressure and could irritate people quite easily. For example, Henry Ford started Chemurgy along with Luther Burbank and Waldo Semon to use agriculture products to make useful plastics and food.

In one instance Ford developed a plastic car from soybeans. That is a plastic derived from soybean starting materials. The car's hood and trunk lid were made from this plastic and with a lot of hoopla Henry Ford showed it off at a Press Conference inviting many leading dignitaries from industry...one of whom was Dr. G. F. D'Alelio. In the presentation Ford took a fire axe and struck the trunk lid a number of times to the amazement of the audience. At that point Dr. D'Alelio called out, "Mr. Ford, why don't you use the sharp point of the axe and not a flat blow?" The audience was stunned, Mr. Ford pissed off and Dr. D'Alelio was never again invited to visit the Ford Motor Company.

The American Chemical Society meetings are big events for chemists around the world and a usual protocol is to designate a large hotel as Convention Headquarters. An example would be the Conrad Hilton in Chicago. After the paper presentations are done for the day, many delegates would congregate in the lobby and it was not unusual to hear calls for telegrams for important people who were milling around. People who were being paged were looked upon as pretty important.

Well it seems that at each ACS meeting there were numerous calls, "Telegram for Dr. Egloff" who was a well known catalyst expert from Universal Oil Products. For some reason, D'Alelio noted the unusual number of telegrams for Dr. Egloff every time they both attended these meetings. So, as in the Ford incident, D'Alelio decided to check into the source of these telegrams, assuming that his company was trying to reach him on some urgent matter.

Well, it turned out that Dr. Egloff had been sending these telegrams to himself to show off his importance.

So if you want to look important, send yourself a telegram.

TIM TEBOW

One of the rising stars in football is Tim Tebow. He has had a great career in high school and college football and now in the National Football League. During his rise to power and fame he has been outspoken in his love for Jesus Christ. During his college days he would display on his eye paint John 3:16 or other bible verse references. This caused an uproar In the secular community and has caused him some unfair criticism for his outward demonstration of his faith in Jesus Christ. At the end of a game he openly expresses his thanks to Jesus, regardless of the press or media.

The other night Denver was playing Chicago and the game was very close. The opportunity for Denver to win this game grew dimmer as the game came to a close. In spite of the great odds against Denver, Tebow was able to direct a drive that tied the game with help of some serious errors committed by the Chicago Bears. Meanwhile, I was rooting for Denver just because of the vilification that Tebow has lived with from secularists.

In thinking about this I realized that God does not care a bit about any sports contest, being more interested in the Salvation of souls, than winning games for any team. Some suggest that Tebow has God on his side, but this is blasphemy to suggest that.

There is however, a good opportunity for Christians to see what Faith in Jesus can do for anyone. Many Christians are shirtsleeve Christians, who when challenged to support their Christian faith, will back down. Consider for example members of congress who claim to be Christian, but back down when they are called upon to stand up for Christian principles. Good examples are the fight against abortion or gay marriage; the latter is an oxymoron.

Jesus warned about the faint hearted when He charged his followers that "If you do not acknowledge me before men, I will not acknowledge you before my Father".

On the internet today, a rabbi denounced Tim Tebow and stated that if Denver were to win the Super Bowl against all odds, Tim's followers would be emboldened to do insane things like burning mosques, bashing gays and immigrants.

So much for the fear that Jesus and people like Tim Tebow strikes in the hardened hearts of the secularists.

"There is nothing more frightening, than ignorance in action"..Goethe

*****

Part III

EDUCATION AND INDUSTRY TALES

ALLYLBENZENE

When Grandpa Bigdog was attending the University of Notre Dame he worked on heterogeneous catalysis trying to understand the mechanism of Ziegler type catalysts for producing polyethylene and polypropylene. The project was full of uncertainty and lots of hard work, but in the end GBD showed that the product of a Ziegler type polymerization was determined by the ratio of the catalyst system: trialkyl aluminum and titanium tetrachloride. At the optimum 1:1 ratio, stereospecific polyethylene or propylene or isoprene were obtained. This finding completed my dissertation work and the last semester at Notre Dame was spent as a Teaching Fellow.

In our laboratory we had several graduate students including Harry White, Leo Mallavarapu, Lewis Taft, George Pezdirtz, Bob Becker and Jim Williams. Dr. D'Alelio, Doc, Research Director, had also invited two Swiss postdoctoral fellows, Dr. Roland Haberli and Dr. Conrad Bruschweiler a.k.a. Dr. Umlaut. Umlaut's project was to attempt to polymerize divinylbenzene with heterogeneous catalysts to polymerize only one double bond leaving the pendant double bond for radiation crosslinking. The project did not go well so Dr. D'Alelio shifted him to studying the polymerization of allylbenzene.

Allylbenzene cannot be prepared into a high polymer because of the activity of the allyl hydrogens adjacent to the double bond. An allyl shift occurs and only oils or brittle resins result. One of the pioneer polymer chemists of the day was C. O. Schildknecht who produced the first stereospecific poly alkylvinyl ethers and was interested in allylbenzene polymerization. So somewhere along the way, Dr. D'Alelio who was a consultant for Foster Grant, was urged to try to polymerize allylbenzene, a project assigned to Umlaut.

Dr. Arnold Finestone was Director of Research for Foster Grant and he and Dr. D'Alelio agreed to present a paper for publication in the Journal of Polymer Science based on Umlaut's work. Meanwhile, Umlaut left town ten minutes ahead of the posse` leaving Doc high and dry. It seems that Umlaut had obtained a job with Imperial Chemical Industries in England. So Doc was stuck.

Lew Taft had just returned from a 2 year service at the Army Chemical Center to continue his research for a Ph.D. Lew had been working on tri-azines, but left when he was drafted. So Doc convinced Lew to help him with a crash project to finish the paper that had been written without exper-imental data. Doc and I had a falling out and I was a teaching fellow so I told him I could not bail him out.

After some strong arguments I finally agreed to help Lew prepare the necessary catalysts based on my dissertation, under the condition that Lew and I would be coauthors. Doc agreed and Lew and I set out to provide the necessary data to complete the paper. The remarkable thing was that solid polyallylbenzene could be prepared at the 1:1 catalyst ratio. [G.F. D'Alelio, A.B. Finestone, L. Taft and T. J. Miranda. J.Poly.Sci. 45, 83 (1960).

So all ended well! This was a great example of what I consider **noon hour research,** where a project is completed with lightning speed under pressing circumstances. Lew went back to his project and we both learned from the experience.

BEHAVIORAL MODIFICATION

When Grandpa Bigdog worked at Whirlpool Dr. Gale Cutler, Director of Research and Engineering, invited him to serve on the Executive Lecture Committee of the Benton Harbor Chamber of Commerce. After the first meeting the Chairman resigned and I inherited the job for the next ten years. The mission of the ELC was to provide executive seminars for managers in area industries. Our committee would discuss current topics in management, recommends an expert then provide a seminar that lasted from lunch to 5:00 p.m. These meetings were well attended and supported by the Chamber of Commerce.

One day we decided to hold a meeting on Behavioral Modification and the best expert on that subject was Dr. D. Chris Anderson who held a Chair and Professor of Psychology at Notre Dame University. His seminar was so good that GBD invited Dr. Anderson to speak at Whirlpool's Annual Sigma XI dinner where he really treated the audience to an excellent after dinner lecture on the subject of BM.

When Father Hesburgh needed six million dollars to complete the library at Notre Dame, he accepted the money from the Rockefellers through the Ford Foundation. Shortly after that things began to change at that former Catholic University. Students were required to wear a tie and jacket to evening meals, attend mass several times a week and prayer preceded each lecture. These rules faded away. Soon faculty would appear in class without a tie or a day or two of unshaven beard. [The idea was to make Notre Dame more like Princeton and those other Eastern schools]. One of the most egregious changes was to make Notre Dame coeducational and this lead to some problems.

Shortly after women were admitted a problem arose in the Chemistry Department. It seems that an elderly professor would stroll back and forth in front of the blackboard rubbing his heart [read genitals] and caused some embarrassment to the young ladies. The students decided to seek help about this behavior and went to see the big BM on campus, Dr. Anderson.

After reviewing the problem, Dr. Anderson suggested some steps to change the behavior without embarrassing the professor. He suggested that the students keep a record of the number of times this behavior occurred during a lecture. So the students began to log the number of heart attacks that occurred each lecture period and reported back to Dr. Anderson.

Numbers like 58, 61, and 57 were common over the observation period. Having this information in hand Dr. Anderson suggested that they devise a behavioral modifier and determine the statistical results. The modifier was simply to have all the students put their heads down on their desks each time a heart attack occurred and record the results of this practice. The averages looked like this; 1, 2, 0 and 3.

"So," said Dr. Anderson, "We have a behavioral modifier, now to verify its effectiveness".

He then asked the students to stop the modifier and again take measurements. The results were 60, 58, 61 verifying the effectiveness of this BM.

So the students returned to their Behavioral Modification mode and the problem was solved.

CHRISTMAS PARTY

When I was Director of Research for the O'Brien Corporation, a paint company, I got involved in the Chicago Society for Paint Technology, later Chicago Society for Coatings Technology. I was asked by Tom Moran, a past president, to run for the Office of Membership Chairman in the Fall Election. Well I figured that who would know Tom Miranda in Chicago and my chances for being elected were slim so I agreed and besides they took nominations from the floor.

The Chicago Society held a monthly meeting at the American Furniture Club in North Chicago and usually had a large attendance since it was the second largest Society in the Federation of Societies for Coatings Technology. During the business meeting the President announced the slate of nominees for the next year and someone leaped up and requested the nominations be closed. So I was elected. I then called the President and asked him if I could decline to run in the next election and he informed me that I would have to go through the chairs...it was a five year stint.

The Furniture Club meeting place was at the top of the building with a large dining room overlooking Lake Michigan and the entire Chicago Skyline. There was a long hallway outside the meeting room and across the hallway were the cloakroom, men's and ladies rooms and a meeting room where the Board of Directors for the Furniture Club met.

Christmas Time.

One of the functions of the Vice President of the Chicago Society was Chairman of the Christmas Party, Golf Outing and Seminars. When I became Vice President, it was my job to organize and develop these functions. The Christmas Party consisted of a fine dinner and entertainment...also arraigned by me and involved hiring dancing girls, comedy acts

126

etc. This party was well attended! (I was also told that the management of the Furniture Club did not allow strippers and I soon found out why.)

It seems that a few years ago, one of my predecessors was Louis Ludwig who worked at Sherwin-Williams in Chicago. As program chairman he had arranged for strippers to perform at the Christmas Party. The strippers would finish their act, they would pick up what little clothes they had and run naked up the hall to the ladies room that was a considerable distance from the meeting room. Well on this particular night the Board of Directors and their wives were having their Christmas Party and we leaving when one of the strippers ran full force into the wives of the Board members.

Needless to say they were no more strippers at the Christmas Party.

HOW BEEG?

When I left the O'Brien Corporation, I became a Staff Scientist at the Whirlpool Corporation. Whirlpool World Headquarters is located in Benton Harbor and their Engineering Center was in St. Joseph, Michigan.

St. Joseph is a small lakeshore town that is a beautiful community where the black population was about 7%, while Benton Harbor, across the St. Joseph River was about 142% black. St. Joseph officials enforced the building codes, while Benton Harbor did not. By contrast Benton Harbor looked like the German tanks had just left ten minutes ago. Homes with broken windows and doors and lot of empty houses left by white flight were a common site.

One day I was asked by Dr. Gale Cutler to drive an official of a German firm to the airport. During our ride he asked me why there was such a difference between the two cities. So I took a detour and drove down Main Street and asked him to look at the large homes lining the street and asked him to count the number of gas meters on each house. On some homes there were 8-10 gas meters. That meant that the welfare department was jamming many families into these large homes and the homes soon became uninhabitable.

The Research and Engineering Center is located on the HQ campus where scientists and engineers had their offices and laboratories. I was in charge of the Materials Science Group, Dr. Don Scherpereel headed the Metallurgy Group and Dr. Richard Ifkovits, the Microbiology Group. Don's office was next to mine and Dick Ifkovits was across the hall.

One of the problems we used to have was unwanted phone calls from the community that went something like this:

[Phone rings]: "Dr. Miranda
[Male voice]: Ah is looking fo the Mayaton Station.
[Dr. Miranda]: This is the Whirlpool Corporation
[Male voice]: Ah lef my car at the Mayaton Station and ah don no which one.
So I looked up some numbers for him and hung up.

[Phone rings]: "Dr. Miranda
[Angry Female voice]: "Willie, where is my pot"
[Dr. Miranda]: This is the Whirlpool Corporation
[Angry Female voice]: Willie, you stole my pot and ah want it back!
[Dr. Miranda]: This is the Whirlpool Corporation
[Angry Female voice]: Willie, you bring back my pot rite now!

One Friday afternoon I heard Dick Ifkovits phone ring and shortly thereafter Dick with a stunned look came into my office to tell me he just had a phone call:

[Phone rings]: "Dr. Ifkovits.
[Female voice with slow drawl]: How beeg is you dick?

I USED TO WORK IN CHICAGO

W hen I was a student at San Jose State College, I worked my way through as a movie projectionist. I had been instrumental in helping the local projectionists organize a union and as a reward I was able to join the union (after paying the usual bribe called an initiation fee), but this was a great ticket to finishing my education.

After the union was formed there was a job opening at the Cinema Theater in Mountain View that showed Mexican films exclusively. Since I did not know Spanish I did not pay much attention to the films except the Newsreels that always concluded with the bull fights.

After a two-year stint at the Cinema, a job opened at the Sunnyvale Theater and I was able to move there. The Sunnyvale Theater was a 1000 seat theater and a more lucrative job paying about $2.25/hr. and I worked there until after graduation from college. One of the union rules directed the projectionist to be paid for thirty minutes prior to the opening of the show. Since the show started at 7:00 pm on week nights, I would be required to be there at 6:30 giving me time to lubricate and clean the projectors, wind film and load the projectors for the evening show. The next task was fifteen minutes prior to the start of the movie I would play recorded music and show advertising slides from local merchants. Then at 7:00 I would start the projector and we were off.

Enter Ole Yancey!

Ole Yancey the doorman and assistant manager was a nice guy. Well one evening as I came in to work he asked me to play a record before the show. So I took the record up and set it on the turntable then went on to preparing the projectors for the show. Well, I forgot to play the record.

About 6:45 the audience began filling the theater and I remembered that I had forgotten to play Ole's record so I turned it on and went about my business loading film into the projectors. I happened to look out the porthole and saw Ole flying up the stairs toward the projection room and pounding on the door.

TURN IT OFF!! TURN IT OFF!!

I could also hear the audience laughing as an embarrassed Ole went back down the stairs to the lobby.

Well, you see, the record he asked me to play was "<u>I USED TO WORK IN CHICAGO</u>" which was a bawdy kind of record you would only play at the American Legion Men's Stag party and something you never played in public.

So much for pre-show music!

INTERVIEW AT GENERAL ELECTRIC

Dr. G. F. D'Alelio was a Distinguished Professor of Chemistry, Head of the Chemistry Department at the University of Notre Dame and my research professor. Doc, as we called him, was a world famous Polymer Pioneer and after graduation from Johns Hopkins University became the Director of Research at General Electric. During his tenure there he was heavily involved in the chemistry of phenol-formaldehyde resins that GE used as insulation material and for varnishes and molded plastic products. After leaving GE Doc was Vice-President for the Pro-phy-lactic Brush Company, Industrial Rayon then at Koppers in Pittsburgh.

Doc was very prolific in seeking patents for his work and when he died had over 600 patents. He was vying to overtake Carlton Ellis who had one thousand patents to his name. One of the men who helped D'Alelio obtain many patents was Dr. Walter Monacelli, who was a Patent Attorney at Koppers.

Meanwhile, Dr. Charles C. Price, a Quaker, was Head of the Chemistry Department at Notre Dame and Father Hesburgh was eager to replace him. (Father Hesburgh also dispatched Dean Clarence Manion, Dean of the Law School and respected Constitutional Lawyer and replaced him with a liberal from Cleveland, Dean O'meara). The Notre Dame Chemistry Faculty, especially Milton Burton, Director of the Radiation Laboratories wanted Dr. Charles Overberger from Brooklyn Polytechnic Institute to replace Dr. Price who later went to the University of Pennsylvania. But , Monacelli was a good friend of Father Joyce who was Vice President of Notre Dame who persuaded Fr. Joyce to hire Doc instead. This would allow Walter and Doc to write many patents being freed from any patent ownership of a corporation. They formed the DAL-MON Corporation to market Doc's patents that Walter would write.

Dr. D'Alelio was a genius, but unfortunately quite outspoken, had only friends and enemies, nothing in between and unfortunately the latter were most numerous. Some of his enemies would go into a rage at the mere mention of his name. His friends like Drs. E. L. Kropa, Calvin Schildnecht and Ray Seymour always spoke highly of Gaetano F. D'Alelio.

One of the big events in Graduate School was near the end, where graduates began to look for employment either in the academic or industrial world. So near the end of our years at Notre Dame we began interviewing companies like Dupont, Rohm and Haas, Dow Chemical, Hercules and oil companies like Shell and Exxon, then ESSO and ENJAY. Lew Taft had interviewing down to a science. He would schedule a number of consecutive interviews so that he would start at Dupont in Delaware and work his way up the East Coast.

Professor Ernest Eliel is an international authority on stereochemistry and had many students' working in this area including Jack Ryan, Zach Hamlet, Mark Rerick and others. One of Dr. Eliel's students interviewed at General Electric and was very well received. After a busy day of interviewing, he looked like cinch to be hired on the spot. At the end of the day they told Dr. Eliel's student that he should meet the Research Director. The student's host introduced him and mentioned that he was graduating from Notre Dame.

"Great", said the Research Director, "That's Charlie Prices' School"
"No" said the student, "Dr. D'Alelio is the Head of the Chemistry Department"
"Who??" he gasped

The Research Director collapsed in his chair and began cursing and burst into a fit of rage as the student's host quickly ushered the embarrassed student out. I never found out if the poor student ever was accepted at General Electric.

LIQUID LITE

After graduating from Notre Dame Grandpa Bigdog became Director of Research for the O'Brien Corporation a paint manufacturer. One of GBD's challenges was to develop new technology for the company to improve our competitive position.

O'Brien's history is long being founded in 1857 in South Bend, Indiana. During the days of horse driven carriages, it took the Studebaker Brothers 28 days to make a Conestoga wagon. The reason for this was the long times required between varnish coats to dry. One day Patrick O'Brien developed a fast drying varnish that shortened the drying time and he called it O'Brien's Electric Primer since it dried faster than competitive varnishes and he started the O'Brien Electric Priming Company. [Electric was a magic word like atomic a century later]. O'Brien became a supplier to Studebaker until the latter's demise.

O'Brien made some other great technical discoveries including Thermalized Tung Oil. Varnishes made from Tung oil were the fastest drying varnishes, but has a disadvantage in gas checking that ruined the finish. Gas checking was caused by the high degree of unsaturation of Tung Oil. Bert Reese, who later became President of O'Brien developed a high temperature process for treating Tung Oil that eliminated the problem.

After World War II, the Dow Chemical Company had a large capacity for making styrene-butadiene latex, a water dispersed emulsion, used to make synthetic rubber. With the end of the war Dow needed a new outlet for this product and developed a water based latex paint that would launch the do-it-yourself market. So Dow officials approached O'Brien to help them develop latex paints, but the people at O'Brien were too short sighted to recognize the enormous benefits from this development. So Dow approached Glidden who was successful and the first to offer water based paint for house paint, Spred Satin.

The result was fantastic and ordinary people could now paint their own walls and wash up the rollers and brushes with water. The latex paints were flat and to do window trim still required oil based semi gloss paint. Other latex bases emerged using vinyl acetate and acrylic monomers that were better than styrene-butadiene. So now the race was on to develop a water based semi-gloss.

GBD started a research program to develop water dispersible polymers. After some time we developed and patented several water soluble polymers and a successful semi-gloss latex and I published a seminal paper on the Chemistry of Water Soluble Polymers. However, the vice president found out that we used a combination of a water soluble alkyd and a Rohm and Haas acrylic emulsion to achieve a semi-gloss paint and insisted we develop a non latex water soluble coating. This was the end of the program since without the latex for fast dry, recoating was impossible because the water soluble coupling agents, butyl cellosolve lifted the previous coat.

Meanwhile, Lori Crisorio, the Technical Rep for Union Carbide [later Vice-President] called GBD to set up a seminar to discuss and demonstrate Carbide's solution. Lori also pointed out that this breakthrough was so exclusive that they were presenting this to O'Brien since we were a large consumer of their products. On the appointed afternoon the Carbide group showed up and put on a dog and pony show emphasizing that we were the first to see this breakthrough.

At the end of the presentation the speaker reached into his brief case and pulled out a quart of paint with the O'Brien Liquid Lite label much to the awe of O'Brien people. Here was the answer and we were the first to see this. He placed the can on the table and we made some small talk when the scotch tape that held the label gave way and the O'Brien label fell off revealing a Sherwin-Williams label that they used in a presentation to S-W earlier in the day.

LIVING HINGE

In the early 1950's there were some remarkable discoveries made in the Polymer Industry. Dr. Karl Ziegler discovered a low- pressure catalyst to make linear polyethylene that stunned the Polymer Industry. His process could be conducted at atmospheric pressure instead of high pressures used at that time. Dr. Ziegler licensed his process to Monticatini in Italy and there Dr. Gulio Natta began a study of using Ziegler catalysts to produce polypropylene. Professor Natta also showed by X-ray analysis that polypropylene (PP) had three structural forms, the isotactic form having the highest melting point and could be used in appliances and automotive applications.

Meanwhile, SUNOCO in Philadelphia began to market PP and its most unusual property of being able to be processed into a living hinge. (If you look at a cosmetic or dental floss box there is a hinge that allows opening and closure over many times, because of the living hinge.) Other companies soon offered PP on the market.

Ford Motor Company was quick to realize the potential of using the living hinge process to make accelerator pedals for their automobiles and ran an extensive campaign touting this new miracle plastic that would replace a more expensive metallic hinge.

Meanwhile, engineers in the Appliance Industry were watching this development and realized that the Living Hinge could be applied to vacuum cleaner switch pedals and in detergent dispensers for dishwashers. Because of isotactic PP's higher melting point, 160° Centigrade it was well suited for dishwasher applications and was used to make sump screens, silverware baskets and pump parts. Soon dishwashers were being produced with PP sump screens and silverware baskets and the great marketing feature of a living hinge detergent dispenser. Marketing people can get very excited when a new feature can be used to promote the sale of a product. This was also true here. Market driven forces can sometimes trump good scientific advice.

Unfortunately, PP is a branched hydrocarbon and very prone to form hydroperoxides that degrade the polymer. In order to prevent oxidation, phenolic stabilizers and inorganic compounds like organo-tin additives are required in small, but expensive amounts.

$$-(-\!\!-CH_2\text{-}CH\!\!-\!\!)_n\text{-} \ + O_2 \qquad = \ -(-\!\!CH\!-\!CH\!\!-\!)_n\!\!-\!\!- $$

with OOH on the upper chain and CH_3 groups below each:

$$\begin{array}{ccc} & & OOH \\ & & | \\ -(-\!-CH_2\text{-}CH\!-\!)_n\text{-} + O_2 & = & -(-CH\!-\!CH\!-\!)_n\!-\!- \\ | & & | \\ CH_3 & & CH_3 \end{array}$$

Meanwhile, back at Ford, there was some concern because the living hinges on their accelerator pedals were dying. The mechanical strength required for this application the gradual loss of stabilizers lead to catastrophic failures and required recall of many automobiles. [Where were the Market Managers who were pushing this when we needed them?]

As the auto industry worked on the problem, surprises were appearing in Laundry Engineering Laboratories. Here too the living hinges were also dying and many engineers would open their morning mail and find pieces of the living hinge enclosed and a letter complaining about unhappy customers. To make matters worse many times whole sump screens and silver ware baskets were crumbling and could be mailed in an envelope to the frustrated engineers.

'Living Hinge' became a forbidden word in Laundry Engineering Laboratories. So much for rushing a break-through products too quickly.

LOOK UNDER THE BED

When Grandpa Bigdog worked at Whirlpool he did a lot of traveling and spent many nights in hotels and motels. GBD stayed in some very nice hotels, Okura in Tokyo, Boca Raton in Boca Raton, Pebble Beach and others. He also stayed in some real dumps like a Motel 6 in Marion, Ohio and the Runnymede in Atlantic City. The Runnymede was where they signed the Magna Carta.

One of the practices GBD made upon entering a hotel room was to look under the bed. So after putting my luggage down, I would look under the bed, check the shower and closets and the locks on the doors. One of the worst hotels in GBD's experience was the Americana Hotel in New York City. GBD had stayed there for American Chemical Society meetings and never liked that Hotel.

One day Dr. Howard Gerhart of PPG invited GBD to speak at a meeting of the National Paint and Coatings Association in New York....and yes, at the Americana Hotel.

So I got a reservation at the hotel and just before leaving Benton Harbor, I asked Linda, our secretary to confirm my hotel room, which she did. On arriving at La Guardia Airport my problems began. First, I had to take a bus to downtown New York and from there take a cab to the Americana. As I was leaving the bus, some good Samaritan grabbed my brief case and told me that he would get me a cab. Well, this thug was on the bus with me and I realized I was scammed. I grabbed my briefcase back and he told me I owed him $3.00 for carrying my bag. He began to curse me and I ducked into a restaurant and eluded him.

I then took a cab to the Americana and was told that I had no reservation. After arguing with the clerk, I finally got a room. The first thing I did

138

was look under the bed and checked the room when I heard someone slipping a key into the lock. GBD kicked the door and heard someone running away.

After this great welcome to New York, GBD went down to a coffee shop and ordered some dinner. Halfway thru dinner some clown threw himself on a stool next to me, lit up a cigarette and placed it under my nose. I quickly paid my bill and left.

Later on I attended a Director of Engineering's Meeting and told some friends about my rule about looking under the bed and about my experience at the Americana. They got a big kick about this. They asked me "what would happen if you found someone under the bed?" I had no answer.

Sometime later at another meeting one of the engineers told me that he too stayed at the Americana and remembered what I said about looking under the bed and he did so. Then he went out to dinner and then went to sleep. During the night he saw a shadowy figure grabbing his wallet and running out the door. What he forgot to do was look under the bed again when he returned from dinner.

One night GBD stayed at a new Marriott Hotel in Columbus, Ohio. As I checked in I put my suitcase on the bed and bent down to look under the bed and **SURPRISE.** There was a face looking at me and I jumped off the floor. When I looked again, I found that they had put mirrors under the bed and I saw my own image and scared the daylights out of me.

So don't forget:

LOOK UNDER THE BED!!!

NO HOPE

After graduating from Notre Dame University Grandpa Bigdog became Director of Research for the O'Brien Corporation in South Bend, Indiana. The company was located on Washington Avenue near the Bendix plant. At the far end of the plant were the alkyd and varnish production and a large storage area for finished alkyd resins.

Just down the street was a bar where they served good Polish food and easily accessible from the rear door of the plant. The Vice President of O'Brien was John C. Mull and he told me an interesting story about that bar.

On Saturday nights they threw a party and most of the clients would show up for food, beer and a good time. [Note: There are no Polish people in heaven; since there is no beer in heaven]. One of John's friends and coworker was Clem Lewandowski who attended the party.

So after a lot of food and beer and after midnight Clem decided to head home since he lived near the plant. So he headed up Orange Street then over to Walnut Street and past the cemetery. Clem then decided to cut through the cemetery as a short cut home. As he stumbled among the gravestones he suddenly fell into a freshly dug grave.

Poor Clem tried to climb out, but it had rained the night before and he couldn't climb up the slippery walls. So the next thing he did was tried shouting but to no avail, so he sat down in a corner of the grave and decided to sit the night out. The next morning someone heard his cries for help and called the fire department to rescue him.

On Monday morning, Clem came to work and told John Mull about his problem over the weekend. John said, "I'll bet you were the most frightened guy in town on Saturday night"

"Well no", said Clem, "I was the second most frightened guy in South Bend".

You see as I was sitting there some drunk fell into the grave and I heard him struggling to get out. After awhile I finally said:

"There is no hope of getting out"

OXIDATION-REDUCTION

After Grandpa Bigdog retired from Whirlpool Corporation, Grandma Bigdog decided to obtain a degree in Music at Indiana University South Bend. GBD was teaching chemistry at that time while GmBD took her courses. Later on GmBD taught piano while still a student. GBD had an old 1984 Corolla that was really rusty, looked like a Filipino taxi, but it belonged to Eddie our dog and he let GBD drive it so he could get a ride. It was funny to pull up to the Music Department to pick up GmBD. She was loaded down with books and Eddie and I would pull up to the stairs and GmBD would pile in. Eddie has the worst looking car on campus. But an old car like this is useful to drive to the Country Club or Church on pledge night.

When GBD taught Chemistry 101 at Indiana University he had some problem teaching the principles of Oxidation-Reduction. Some students understood very easily, but others had a problem so it was important to keep their attention during the lecture and pose some memorable image to help them with recall.

Oxidation is a chemical process in which electrons are lost from an atom, while reduction is a process whereby an atom acquires electrons. A good example is the rusting of iron. In this case iron loses electrons while oxygen acquires electrons to form iron oxide. So when GBD taught this subject, he took the picture of Eddie and set in on the lecture table. The students immediately asked it that was my dog arousing an interest in Eddie. So in the course of the lecture I told them about Eddie's car and how rusty it was. This I told them was because of an oxidation-reduction going on with the iron and oxygen to form iron oxide (rust).

So on the final examination I included this question: Explain Oxidation-Reduction

You can't imagine how many answers went like this: Oxidation is a process where electrons are lost and reduction is where an atom gains electrons, **LIKE EDDIE'S CAR.**

SCHWAN SONG

One of the nice things about the Christmas Season is the activities that emerge and the attitudes of people as we approach this major Federal Holiday Christmas Day that honors the birth of the Savior of the World, Jesus Christ. As November ends we find music in stores and on the air related to various Christmas themes like Christmas carols and various songs and related to the season.

As Christmas approached people gather their wish lists and make decisions regarding whom to send cards or gifts, while decorating the homes inside and out to reflect in the beauty of the season. In our case my job is to make cookies and to bake bread. A delightful way to celebrate the season is to send cookies to friends and family.

Frozen foods and desserts are very helpful to meet the constraints of entertaining. One of the large worldwide food companies is the Schwan Food Company that is a private multibillion dollar firm that sells ice cream, pizza and other high quality food products. Their products are found worldwide in stores and through a marketing plan that delivers their products directly to the home. Their ice cream is really delicious.

We have used the retail service of the Schwan Food Company over the years and have had a lot of different servicemen deliver the product. The Schwan truck is easily identified by the logo on the trucks which are refrigerated to protect the quality of their goods. The task of being a retail distribution driver must be very taxing because the rate of turnover appears to be high; at least in our area.

The last driver we had was a jolly fellow named Arthur. In addition to being very capable of selling Schwan he also had a strong political bent toward the conservative side. In fact, Arthur would make Attila the Hun look like a Gulfstream Liberal. After completing the sale, he would go off into a political rant concerning some issue and we would spend some time listening to his analysis. He would also drop off little bits of political information most of which I was in agreement. So we had a good time taking our congress to the verbal woodshed.

One Christmas season Arthur stopped to drop off some items we had ordered and we gave him a plate of cookies. His next visit was during Christmas week and he stopped by with our order and under his arm he had a large book full of church hymns and Christmas carols. He also had a cold and a bad cough. He explained that he had no gifts for his customers, but decided to sing some carols to his good customers.

So Arthur opened his book and Carol took our order and left me standing alone in our foyer as an audience of one.

Arthur: (cough, cough) God Bless you (cough, cough, cough) merry gentlemen (cough, cough, cough).

Meanwhile, Carol felt sorry for me and decided to come back increasing the audience by 100%.

Arthur: (cough, cough) We three (cough, cough, cough) Kings of Orient (cough) are (cough, cough, cough) bearing gifts (cough, cough). You get the idea.

Well after stumbling through a few more carols he wished us a Merry (cough) Christmas and was on his way.

PHIL'S REMEDY

Grandpa Bigdog had a number of different jobs growing up and later in life. My earliest job was cutting Mrs. Cosme's grass on Awaiolimu Street in Honolulu. Later I used to milk cows for my Uncle Joe who we called Double Rope. When GBD moved to California his first job was as a retail executive at Sprouse-Reitz 5& 10 cents store. After that I became a motion picture projectionist, an electrician at Drew's Cannery, a college teacher, then a Research Director after graduation from Notre Dame University.

Other jobs that GBD held include being a Staff Scientist at Whirlpool Corporation, a Technical Editor for the Journal of Coatings Technology and finally an Adjunct Professor at Indiana University. In this last position GBD taught several chemistry courses including Polymer Chemistry.

One of GBD's favorite course was CHEM 101 Elementary Chemistry, a beginning course for chemistry majors and a very important course in chemistry. This course is so important that at the University of California all major professors are required to teach Elementary Chemistry. Imagine a freshman at California, Berkeley having a Nobel Laureate teaching chemistry. This was a policy started by Professor Gilbert N. Lewis a very famous chemist and teacher.

One of the things GBD did to keep the student's interest was to tell stories during the course of the lecture to illustrate a point or a chemical principle. This he did several times during the course of a lecture and the students seemed to appreciate and remember the good stories long after the semester was over.

GBD's good neighbor is Philip Hunter. Phil is a retired electrical contractor and has a lot of good common sense. GBD likes to take our dog

WAKE over to visit Phil and Jeanne several times a week. Wake likes Jeanne and Phil and gets excited when she knows were going over to see Phil and Jeanne.

On one of our visits I told Phil that I was having trouble with heartburn and sometimes ran out of antacid. Phil responded by telling me to use "Pickle Juice". He takes a tablespoon of pickle liquid to quell a heartburn attack. GBD did not think much of the idea, but one night I ran out of antacid and tried Phil's Remedy and it worked.

So when GBD got to the chapter on Acids and Bases, he found a great opportunity to tell this story to the students. This involves pH, a measure of the strength of acids or bases. Also involved is the use of buffers which can change the equilibrium between different levels of acid or base. Buffers are very important in body chemistry, the stomach is acidic and the ocean is basic (or alkaline). Buffers can modify swings in pH. These include acetate, citrate or phosphate anions.

So Phil's Remedy made a lot of sense, since taking "Pickle Juice" that contains acetate anions, an excellent buffer reduces heartburn. This was also great since it added another story to GBD's list of tales to interest the students.

PLANT TOUR

When Grandpa Bigdog graduated from Notre Dame, he became Director of Research for the O'Brien Corporation, a privately held Paint company started by Patrick O'Brien as the Electric Priming Company in 1857. At the time GBD worked there, 1959-1968 the President of the company was Jerome J. Crowley, Jr. who was also a Notre Dame graduate and later became a member of the Board of Trustees at Notre Dame University.

The O'Brien plant was very old and consisted of several buildings containing different functions. The main building housed the administration and sales offices that connected to the laboratory and faced West Washington Street. Across from the main building was the Lacquer Building. This was a very dangerous place to work since they formulated nitrocellulose lacquers made from gun cotton that is used to fire large cannon and extremely explosive. Another large building housed the varnish works and the alkyd and emulsion reactors, and next was the varnish storage building and solvent storage tanks.

As one would leave the alkyd building to enter the varnish storage area the first thing one would see was the foreman's desk and a telephone. But more significantly this was a great visiting area for some of the scholars who worked at O'Brien because the foreman was an art connoisseur who displayed his museum pieces on the large fire door at the entrance of the varnish building.

At the entrance to the Main Office was a reception area. The telephone operator was Bonnie Mabry, a widow who was very interested in her work and diligent in tracking down anyone who was required to answer the phone. Now Jerry Crowley was a very frugal man (read cheap) and limited the number of phones around the building [for example GBD did not obtain a desk phone until he was there for a year] such that people were regularly paged and would have to go to the nearest phone, call Bonnie and she would connect the parties. As a result during the day we were constantly barraged by Bonnie's voice shouting for someone.

During one summer session at Notre Dame, Dr. G. F. D'Alelio taught a class in Industrial Polymers and many nuns took that class as part of their continuing education. During the course of the semester, he covered paint manufacturing and suggested that some of the nuns should take a tour of the O'Brien factory. So Doc called Jerry Crowley and set up a tour and Jerry was delighted to act as tour guide.

He took the nuns through the laboratory to show them the Industrial Finishing, Architectural and Metal Decorating labs, then on to the varnish building to see how Marine Varnishes and alkyds were prepared. From there they were heading to the paint manufacturing area and as Jerry walked past the Varnish Storage area Bonnie called out, "Mr. Crowley, Telephone". So Jerry led his group of nuns into the museum area as he answered the phone. The nuns were treated to a full size nude and the rest of the nudes in the museum.

There is nothing like a field trip to emphasize what we learn in class.

QUANTITATIVE ANALYSIS

When Grandpa Bigdog attended San Jose State College in the late forties, the college had a quarter instead of a semester system. Elementary Chemistry was divided into 3 quarters; Chemistry 1A, 1B and 1C which included Qualitative Analysis a course requiring the identification of cations and anions, but not the amount of each. For example, a student would be given an unknown containing silver, lead and mercury and would be required to separate the cations and identify each by precipitation. In the case of a silver ion, addition of chloride anion would form a white precipitate. Lead could be separated by hot water then adding sulfuric acid or hydrogen sulfide to form a white precipitate of lead sulfate or lead sulfide. Mercury could also be identified by forming the sulfide, using hydrogen sulfide gas. Hydrogen sulfide gas was piped into the lab and many times students forgot to turn off the gas valves and the lab really smelled bad like rotten eggs.

The next hurdle was Quantitative Analysis, Chemistry 10A,B,C that was taught by a very beautiful Dr. Gertrude Witherspoon (later Cavins), and she was really tough, but not the world's greatest chemist. She was the bane of medical students who needed this course. One of my friends Harold Sebring preceded me in the course and spent no little time telling us how terrible the course was and in some ways he was correct, the major stumbling block was the balance shown above among other problems to be discussed in this tale.

The Balance Room

In those days we did not have magnetic damping or automatic balances so we spent many hours watching the needle swings as the balance pans rocked over the knife-point.. What was more aggravating was if someone entered the balance room when we had an opened window on the balance, the pans would begin to swing or the little milligram rider at the top of the balance would fall off. This would require carefully picking up the rider with tweezers and placing it back on the scale. One of the prerequisites for Quant was a working fluency in profanity because there was a lot of opportunity to use this second language.

Titration

The Quant lab consisted of rows of laboratory benches with utilities in the center and shelves above that will play a part in this story. The upper shelves contained the usual bottles of acids and bases and space for books and two 2 ½ liter bottles containing standard acid and base. At one end of the lab were drying ovens and furnaces to drive water from porcelain crucibles. In an adjoining room were the notorious balances where we spent most of our time weighing samples.

The first quarter was devoted to titration and our first chore (hazard) was to prepare two bottles of standard HCl and NaOH. We would take HCl that was 36 normal and dilute it to 0.1 normal using a volumetric flask. We would weigh out the proper amount of NaOH to make a 0.1 normal solution. In those days we used normality instead of molarity that in the case of these two chemicals are identical. Preparing the solutions was not too difficult, but placing them into the 2 ½ liter bottles presented a hazard. First we needed to prepare glass tubes and bend them so that we could siphon the acid or base from the shelf above. This is where every quarter at least one student would be injured by forcing the glass tubing into a rubber stopper where the glass would break and end up in palm of the students hand. We also had to protect the NaOH solution from absorbing carbon dioxide so we attached a tube of calcium chloride to the air inlet to absorb carbon dioxide. [This was before Al Gore so we did not have to worry about this dangerous gas that the Supreme (?) Court has now determined to be a pollutant].

After we had prepared our standard solutions we had to standardize them. For example, HCl would be standardized with sodium carbonate. Sounds simple but it wasn't. First we had to prepare fresh N_2CO_3 from sodium bicarbonate. This is where the time consuming problem began. First we had to weigh a crucible then place it in a furnace and dry it to constant weight, required several trips to the balance room and the hazard of removing a red-hot crucible and placing it into a dessicator to dry. The usual difficulty here was that after the crucibles were placed into the dessicator and the cover restored to the dessicator, students carried the dessicator to their desks as the hot crucibles raised the internal pressure inside the dessicator and the lid would pop off, crashing to the floor into many pieces. [We shall return to this problem later.]

Unlike modern laboratories, we did not have burets with teflon® stopcocks or automatic pipets. Our burets were calibrated, open on top and a taper at the bottom to fix a rubber tube containing a glass bead that acted as a valve when squeezed. A major problem was that the valve would leak or overshoot the endpoint requiring repeating the procedure.

The Lecture

Dr. Witherspoon would waltz around the lecture table wearing her knit dresses that at times could be distracting for the male students as various three dimensional shapes would accompany her lectures. She also was not the greatest teacher especially when it came to topics like molarity, equilibrium, and balancing oxidation-reduction equations. So whenever we came to a tough part, she was out of town and either Ray Wilkerson or Dr. Benjamin Naylor would step in and provide the information we needed. Dr. Naylor, who taught Physical chemistry was also head of the Chemistry Department and a great teacher and we learned what Dr. Witherspoon couldn't quite get over to us.

There were two interesting students in our class, John Harstock and a former sergeant in the Woman's Army Corps named Martha. John was a nice guy and very eager student whose lab spot was opposite the WAC's spot. She had a foul mouth, but perfect for the balance room and was always borrowing glassware from me, returning them in shards of glass because she would drop them. Whenever we had our tests returned we could always count on Martha's fluency in profanity to be demonstrated. All in all she should have never been allowed in a chemistry lab.

Chemistry 10B

Having survived the first quarter, most of the students realized that in order to complete the course in time we would have to get a jump-start on weighing techniques and how to reduce time spent in the balance room. The second quarter involved gravimetric analysis including iron ore analysis and Kjeldahl analysis of nitrogen.

For the iron analysis we had to weigh porcelain crucibles to constant weight that required heating the crucibles to red heat, cooling in the dessicator and reweighing. While this was going on we prepared our usual standard solutions for titrations.

For some reason John Harstock got the jump on everyone. He had prepared and standardized his solutions, and had dried his crucibles to constant weight long before anyone else. He was well into his iron analysis until he met up with **Black Tuesday!**

One Tuesday morning John came charging into the lab and opened his locker to retrieve a 1000 ml volumetric flask. As he pulled the flask out, he hit the side of the dessicator and broke the flask. He then retrieved the dessicator and carried it over to the furnace where his iron oxide samples had been fired and he placed them in the dessicator. As he carried the dessicator to his lab bench the lid blew off and as he reached for the lid the bottom of the dessicator with his samples crashed to the floor breaking the crucbles and dessicator. Just then Martha came into the lab and put her books up on the shelf and knocked his two 2 ½ liter standard solutions down breaking both. Dr. Cavins came over to John and told him he had better go home. So he grabbed his books and headed for the door as his momentum caused his expensive slide rule out of its case smashing the glass on the slide rule.

John was back to square ONE.

RADIO OR PHYSICAL CHEMISTRY?

One of the problems young people face is making important career decisions that can have a life long impact. Making the wrong decision can be disastrous and have long-term consequences. That is why a young person should think things over seriously and even consult with others who can help make the correct career choice.

When I was finishing my junior year at San Jose State College, I needed to make a decision regarding Physical Chemistry that was a full year course. I had also toyed with the idea of studying Radio instead since my friend Ralph McKee was doing that and spoke highly of the course. [Ralph later joined the Air Force and eventually became a General]. The idea behind studying Radio was so I could get a job in the Merchant Marine as a radio operator and see the world. Such are the dreams of young people who are not fully informed.

One of my high school friends was Harold Fairchild who was on the track team with me, Merrill Grim and Mac Martin. After graduation Harold took some courses at San Jose State off and on. He also joined the Merchant Marine and came back with stories of the places he had visited on his long absences. Harold had obtained a job as a wiper in the engine room. This job required that he kept after oil spills and looked after lubrication chores as required in the engine room.

So now it is decision time, should I take Radio or Physical Chemistry? I talked to some friends about it but could not make a rational decision until I realized that the best way to find out was to talk to Harold Fairchild. Harold's father owned a drug store in Campbell so I went there to inquire when Harold would be back in town. After learning the date I eagerly awaited his return from Hong Kong so I could ask about opportunities in the Merchant Marine.

One evening I trotted over to Harold's home eager to learn about the world of the Merchant Marine and the adventures of his last voyage. After a while I mentioned to Harold my plan to study Radio so I could get into the Merchant Marine. I then asked Harold a few questions to get some good background information:

Tom: **Have you ever been to London?**
Harold: Yes, the whorehouses are about two blocks from the dock.
Tom: **Have you ever been to Hamburg?**
Harold: The whorehouses are about four blocks from the docks.
Tom: **Did you ever go to Singapore?**
Harold: The whorehouses are right near the docks.

So apparently Harold had seen the world through a whorehouse window and that made an easy decision for me so I enrolled in Physical Chemistry and that was a better choice.

ROCKFORD VARNISH

Grandpa Bigdog worked in the paint industry for many years, nine years making paint and 23 years as a user of paint at the Whirlpool Corporation. Paint manufacture involves a number of technologies including Polymer Chemistry, Pigment technology, Solvents, Additives, Formulation and Analytical Chemistry. Each of these contribute to the value of the end product whether it be house paint, automobile coatings, marine finishes, aircraft coatings and container coatings to mention a few.

As the Coatings Industry evolved new technologies emerge constantly and those actively participating in the industry must remain informed by further study, reading journals and trade literature and attending coating conferences where short courses are offered.

During GPD's tenure there were a number of journals and magazines devoted to the industry; some required subscription like the Journal of Coatings Technology and the American Paint Journal. Others like PAINT AND VARNISH PRODUCTION, PRODUCT FINISHING and others were offered free by simply filling out a card, signing and the magazine would be shipped regularly. In the free magazines many of the articles would be written by people who worked in supplier's laboratories that described a new resin, pigment or additive and compared their product to others in the field such as exterior exposure, corrosion protection and other issues germane to the coatings specialist.

GBD was Technical Editor of the Journal of Coatings Technology for twenty years and this was refereed journal such that we did not accept papers promoting a particular product. The JCT was more scientifically oriented, with related articles set aside from the technical ones.

The free publications usually arrived at a certain day and many of the scholars, especially in the varnish department eagerly awaited the arrival of the PRODUCT FINISHING issue. It was interesting to walk through the varnish department when PF arrived. The scholars who read it would immediately strip off the mailing cover and immediately flip through to the index page that was the most important page in each issue. Then there would either be a big smile or a look of sadness depending on whether the **Rockford Varnish** ad was included which was included every other week.

What was so important about the RV ad? Well the RV ad had a nude model in about every other issue and these were quickly scanned, cut out and posted in the locker of the varnish room scholars for further study.

Continuing education has its benefits.

TAKE 'EM ALL

When Grandpa Bigdog graduated from the University of Notre Dame in 1959, he became Director of Research for the O'Brien Corporation a paint company founded in South Bend, Indiana by Patrick O'Brien. Patrick O'Brien worked for the Studebaker Brothers in South Bend who manufactured Conestoga wagons and later automobiles. The process for making a wagon required 28 days because the varnishes took a long time to dry. O'Brien developed a fast drying varnish and started the Electric Priming Company on West Washington Avenue. At the time of his invention, Electric had the same impact as Atomic did in the late 1940's.

Members of the O'Brien family and later the Crowley family lead the company until a period when Jerome Crowley, Jr. was not quite ready for the leadership role. Bert Reese was asked to head the company until Jerry Crowley was in a position to take over.

During the period after World War I varnish drying was a long-term process because the reaction rate between oxygen of the air and the varnish, usually linseed or soybean oil, was slow. The fastest drying oil was Tung oil obtained from the Tung nut in China. Tung oil contains three conjugated unsaturation sites that favor faster drying of varnishes and superior varnish properties. However, Tung oil varnishes have an unfavorable after effect; where the clear film would fog up after drying ruining furniture or floors. This is called gas checking

Many attempts were made to overcome this problem and it was Bert Reese who solved the problem by heating the oil to over 750 ° F for about 90 seconds and quenching the hot oil. O'Brien obtained a patent on their new Thermalized Tung Oil. This was a real breakthrough technology in the paint industry.

One of Bert's collaborators was Matthew Taggart. Matt was a very smart man and well versed in varnish technology. Matt had a very high vapor pressure and took great pleasure in embarrassing or humiliating people lower in status than he, meaning just about everyone. When I told my family doctor I was going to work for the O'Brien Corporation, he warned me to watch out for Matt Taggart. I soon found out that Dr. Frith was right.

Also working with Matt was John C. Lauder a metal decorating expert from Rinshed-Mason in Detroit and Howard.Roedl, the alkyd chemist who developed and serviced the alkyd production. Alkyd resins were the workhorse of the paint industry and were developed in 1926 by Dr. Roy Kienle at General Electric.

Matt used to like to point out to anyone how many patents he had and that he was a personal friend of Dr. Waldo Semon who developed the plasticizer for polyvinylchloride. Waldo Semon worked with Henry Ford and Luther Burbank to develop the science of CHEMURGY that is making chemicals from agricultural products.

Howard worked with Matt and John Lauder trying to copy alkyds used in the industry. One of the major problems at this time was that alkyd chemists did not quite understand the functionality concept developed by Dr.Wallace H. Carothers at DuPont, the discoverer of nylon. As a result many of the reactions would gel in the glass flasks and Matt would invite Howard to clean the flasks. Generally, the alkyds contain glycerine, phthalic anhydride and an oil. So Matt suggested to Howard that he use concentrated nitric and sulfuric acid to clean the flasks. So Howard would add the acids and began heating the flask over a burner. Recalling his chemistry in Montana State, Howard recalled that when you add these acids to glycerine nitroglycerine was obtained. Howard quickly stopped using this cleaning method.

Another fiasco courtesy of Matt Taggart was in the field of consulting. One day Bert Reese bought a new English car. In those days methyl alcohol was added to prevent freezing in the radiator, but methyl alcohol had a low boiling point and was easily lost from the cooling system. So Bert asked Matt if he had a solution and he recommended butyl alcohol that has a much higher boiling point. So Bert had Matt add butanol to his radiator and drove to Chicago. Well the result was disastrous. First, butanol has a very foul odor and when heated with water will azeotrope and evaporate providing the driver and his passengers with a very foul atmosphere.

Bert was not too happy with Matt and his consulting skills. It also ruined the engine.

Howard Roedl was one of the best alkyd chemists in the industry, but he was an ordained moocher. For example, at any given congregation of people Howard would make a habit of bumming cigarettes from his friends. Well, one day at a large gathering Matt was holding Fort telling people how great he was when Howard came up to Matt and asked him for a cigarette. What poor Howard did not know was that he had granted Matt the perfect opportunity to humiliate him. With a loud voice Matt announced: "**HERE. TAKE 'EM ALL**" What Howard failed to realize was that Matt deliberately carried an unopened pack for just such an occasion.

Well, one day Howard decided to return the favor. He bought a new pack of cigarettes and attended an O'Brien function involving customers and salesmen as well as laboratory staff. As usual Matt was holding Fort with a large group of people. Howard walked past Matt and Matt grabbed his arm and asked for a cigarette.

THIS WAS HOWARD'S BIG DAY!

"HERE. TAKE 'EM ALL"

"No, No", said Matt, "I only want one"

By this time Howard was long gone and Matt looked pretty stupid holding a fresh pack of Camels.

TALL OIL

When Grandpa Bigdog was Vice-President of the Chicago Society for Coatings Technology [CSCT] he was also the Program Chairman. This important post required that GBD provide the programs for the monthly meetings, the Golf Outing and the Christmas Party. The monthly meetings were held in the American Furniture Mart on Chicago's Northside. The meeting room was on the top floor overlooking the Chicago skyline and Lake Michigan.

In order to make more efficiency of member's time the meeting committee agreed to provide two lectures on meeting nights, the first starting at 5:00 pm and the second would be the after dinner speaker on a subject related to Paint or Polymer Chemistry. Usually suppliers like DuPont, Glidden, Titanium Pigments or Baker Castor Oil provided speakers or we would obtain speakers from the Paint companies that made up the CSCT.

During the afternoon, the Executive Committee would meet until about 5 pm when the pre-dinner speech was presented. This presentation was usually more technical where subjects like Thermosetting Acrylics or Crosslinking agents were the fare. This was followed by a social hour, then dinner, the business meeting where the VP would announce the next meeting; then the after dinner presentation.

The attendance at these meetings was very good. Companies like Sherwin-Williams, Glidden, DeSoto, PPG and DuPont paid the dues for laboratory people and this gave them an opportunity for continuing education, meeting others in the industry and most important receiving the largesse of free drinks from the many sales representatives who picked up the drink tabs. As a result by the time the after dinner speech was delivered most of the attendees were far above the legal limit for ethanol. The fallout was that the poor speaker had a difficult time trying to keep these drunks awake.

One evening we had a presentation on Tall Oil. [I won't mention the company to protect the reputation of the guilty.] So GBD got up after dinner and introduced the speaker and he proceeded to tell us about Tall Oil. The talk went like this:

Slide One: Tall Oil and its Applications. [Yawn, Yawn]
Slide Two: Tall Oil comes from the pine tree, Swedish word for pine oil is Tallolja. (In the U. S. pine oil that is a different product so they called it Tall Oil for differentiation. [Yawn, Yawn]
Slide Three: A distillation column for separation of tall oil and rosin. [Yawn, Yawn]
Slide Four: Tall oil is obtained from the Kraft Paper process. [Yawn, Yawn]
Slide Five: Frontal view of nude model!
You never saw an audience spring to life like this one.
Slide Six: Composition of Tall Oil. [Everyone awake anticipating next slide.]
Slide Seven: Side view of two nude models. [Everyone now wide awake]
Slide Eight: A typical alkyd formulation. [What's on the next slide????]
Slide Nine: Three nude models. [WOW].

As you can imagine this went on for some time and the speaker received a great round of applause, but I don't think anyone remembered anything about Tall Oil.

THE ANNOUNCEMENT

An announcement conveys a message that the sender wishes to deliver to a specific or general audience. Usually the information can be brief i.e. FIRE or "He is Risen" or it can be a long detailed announcement like a major catastrophe, "SUNAMI HITS INDONESIA" along with a week or two of follow up until the story is driven from the front pages by emerging announcements.

An announcement can also trigger a trained action. When Uncle Paul's ship was attacked off Samar and General Quarters sounded, the crew immediately sprang into action and prepared to attack an overwhelming force of enemy battleships and cruisers. Recent TV junk shows like the Trump show emphasizes a two word phrase with a lot of impact and follow up: **YOU'RE FIRED!**

In the sports world we encounter announcements that convey a lot of information and triggers actions or reactions like: **TOUCHDOWN!** Such an announcement can trigger a roar of thousands of people in the stands reacting to the news. So all in all announcements play a significant role in our daily activities, let me tell you about a significant announcement that I received when I lived in Campbell, California.

We lived on Foote Street along the Southern Pacific Railroad tracks that lay parallel to Drew's Cannery. Across Campbell Avenue were Dillon Avenue and its surroundings, where many Okies lived. Jack Vitale lived on Dillon Avenue too.

You may remember Jack, the hero of the Train Coming story, who drove his 1938 Dodge sedan down the railroad tracks right into an oncoming train. Jack was a war hero who saved his squadron in Italy from a vicious machine gun attack. Jack also had a booming voice that could wake the dead. He would go the theater and talk during the movies and his voice carried all over above the picture sound. So if Jack was around you could sure tell it was Jack.

We used to go to St. Lucy's Church in Campbell and usually sat in the back so we were the last in and first out. The entrance to the church had a staircase that you would have to ascend to get in and usually many people gathered outside after church on the landing or below at street level. The landing was an ideal place to make an announcement that no one could miss.

One Sunday, Uncle Paul, Merrill Grim, Harold and Bob Fairchild and GBD were standing out on the street. Mrs Grim, Auntie Nellie, Mrs. Suto and many ladies from the church were coming out when Jack appeared at the door of the church to make an announcement to Uncle Paul and soon to be terrified churchgoers.

Jack shouted, "Hey, Paul, I got a piece of ass last night"

Uncle Paul and GBD ducked behind a hedge, the devout ladies were all shocked and the rest of the guys scattered and Jack just stood there as if he were the invited speaker.

So you see the importance and impact of an **announcement!**

THE DATE

After graduation from Campbell High School, Grandpa Bigdog had no idea what to do next. GBD was a projectionist at the Campbell Theater and also worked at Hunt's Foods as an electrician. Hunt's Foods bought out Drew's Cannery that summer. Most of my friends went off to the army so I was rather lost, so I decided to attend San Jose State College.

Since World War II ended many former GI's who had the GI Bill, started college and they were very serious about their studies, while the young freshmen like me were more party oriented. GBD soon learned that the competition was real tough.

One of the ex GI's that I met was Tom Lauret, who majored in Entomology, and we became good friends. Tom had a peculiar trait since he had the Midas Touch; i. e. everything he touched turned to shit as you will soon see. Tom also had a penchant to be attracted to the homeliest looking girls that he would rave about. There was one exception however, when he met Phyllis. She was very pretty and Tom did everything he could to get her attention.

Tom and Phyllis were in the same entomology class and here was where Tom made his big move (read blunder). The class was scheduled for a field trip so Tom asked Phyllis if he could drive her to the trip, to which she agreed. Tom was in seventh heaven because this would give him an opportunity to get to know Phyllis better. So he agreed to pick her up in front of the Science Building at one o'clock.

As Tom pulled up to the Science Building in his 1938 Dodge sedan, he was stunned to see Phyllis with three of her girl friends from class whom she invited to join them. As they drove along the Bay Shore Highway, the women were in constant conversation and Tom was relegated to the position of a cab driver. Tom had to act fast so he tried a ruse to turn the conversation back to him. As they passed a field Tom spotted an Australian Coddling Moth and he shouted:

"Look, an Australian Coddling Moth!!"

The women looked and turned back with disgust. What Tom did not see were two dogs in the act of making more dogs, so Tom was speechless for the rest of the trip. So on the way back the women were again engaged in constant chatter and Tom, who had not learned from the previous blunder and sought another attention grabbing sight. There was a large tarantula spider web between two power poles and Tom called out again. Again Tom failed to see a large stallion in the field in an extended mode.

Well eventually Tom turned his attention to my sister Lorraine, who couldn't care less, but Tom was persistent. He invited her on a date every chance he could, but she refused. Well, one day in late January, Tom mentioned to Lorraine that the Saratoga Theater was showing a foreign film and he wanted to take her there. Lorraine agreed. After the movie Tom and Lorraine approached the car and failed to see a fresh pile of processed dog food as he opened the door for Lorraine. Tom said, "Damn" and proceeded to the rear of the car where Lorraine heard him scraping his shoes on the rear bumper. As they drove away the essence of processed dog food overwhelmed them. Tom stopped the car and did a barnyard shuffle to no avail.

"Do you want to get a hamburger?" asked Tom. "No, take me home" was the reply.

Like King Midas Tom should be in the history books.

TRADEMARKS

The United States Patent was established by Congress to protect intellectual property such as patents, designs and trademarks. Many firms go through a lot of effort to protect their patents from infringement. In pharmaceuticals, polymer technology, coatings and engineering innovations we find many lawsuits in the courts to protect their rights.

American Cyanamid owned a drug division in New Jersey. Many years ago, a chemist named Dr. Robert Aries worked for Lederle . He was a hard working individual (read crook) and would work nights and weekends on antibiotics. Some of the antibiotics he was involved with were the tetracyclines and Lederle had exclusive patents on the cultures and manufactures of these antibiotics.

Well, hard work eventually paid off. One day Lederle found that some of their cultures were stolen. It seems that Dr Aries was smuggling these out at night or on weekends. He then sold these to an Italian pharmaceutical firm which began to manufacture the antibiotics in competition with Lederle. In fact, the Italian prices were so much lower that the U. S. Army began to purchase their antibiotics from Italy, much to the dismay of Lederle.

Our hard worker was arrested and convicted of fraud and theft, but jumped bail and left the country and moved to Monaco. While in Monaco, he learned that there was no extradition treaty with the United States, so he felt safe there.

He then embarked on a new career. He began to obtain Trademark copyrights to all the names and symbols he could think of in the name of the company he formed, much to the dismay of many established firms.

Enter Standard Oil of New Jersey. Standard oil had two trademarks; ESSO and ENJAY. The former was the corporate logo and the latter was for their chemical subsidiary. Well, ESSO decided to develop a new symbol and hired a firm to research a unique symbol which was not copyrighted and could be used worldwide.

SURPRISE! SURPRISE!

ESSO finally settled on EXXON and began a huge public relations blitz to announce their new name (logo). One day executives at EXXON received a registered letter from Robert Aries Associates congratulating them on selecting their copyrighted trademark name and announced the royalty schedule and money due Aries.

EXXON officials were livid over this unfortunate turn of events.

I don't believe that Dr. Aries will be invited to any EXXON functions or to this country.

WHERE'S BUMONT?

When Grandpa Bigdog was in the Army during the Korean post war period he was in the Chemical Corps stationed at the Army Chemical Center, Edgewood, Maryland. The Army has a special classification for people with special skills called Scientific Professional Personnel, (SPP). This meant that instead of peeling potatoes or standing guard, SPP's worked in laboratories or other facilities matching their specialties.

There were several detachments at this post including regular army and SPP's. This facility also manufactured nerve gas and did research on nerve gas and its physiological properties as well as working on antidotes for nerve gas. Since nerve gas was so deadly, all personnel on the post were required to undergo routine cholinesterase tests. Once GBD was accidentally exposed to nerve gas and my cholinesterase level went to zero!

I was assigned to Detachment 3. In another detachment were the regular army personnel including the **MILITARY POLICE.** The regular army people did not care much for the SPP's and the military police were always on the lookout for any violations that they could pin on us; most notably were speeding tickets.

I worked in the Clinical Investigation Laboratory and it was here that we conducted all cholinesterase tests for the post. Sergeant Winston Teal conducted these tests until his term of duty expired and he returned to Texas. The test consisted of a simple pinprick on the edge of a finger to extract a small amount of blood for the test.

Enter Jack Beaumont!

Jack was quite a character. He had attended Florida State and had a degree in microbiology and took over the cholinesterase tests. Jack had another avocation....getting into trouble. He would call in on Monday morning from some local jail asking us to bail him out for some weekend infraction. His other problem came from crossing the trail of a rather pesky MP who had given him two speeding tickets. One more ticket and his car could not be driven on the post again. And this MP was hounding Jack with a vengeance.

One day we were hanging around the lab and Jack was telling us about his troubles with this particular MP when I received a call from the office. I left the group discussion and walked up to the front office to find this obnoxious MP standing there.

"Where's Jack Bumont?" he asked.

"Ahm here to get a test" he admitted.

So I escorted him back to Jack's lab and told him to wait there. Then I walked back and told Jack that his favorite MP was waiting for a cholinesterase test. This was Jack's big chance to get even. So Jack walked into his lab as his favorite MP stood there in full dress garb. Jack reached into a drawer and removed a 250 cc syringe and fitted a stainless steel stopcock onto the syringe. Then he fitted an 8-inch needle onto the stopcock. At this point the MP fainted.

WRONG TURN-RIGHT PATH

One of my favorite books in my library is Psycho-Cybernetics by Dr. Maxwell Maltz. His basic tenet in the book is that one can control success or failure by using the subconscious mind in accomplishing a task or reaching a goal. For example if one considers at task or goal to be impossible, then the subconscious mind will program the conscious mind to a failure path. On the other hand, if one decides that the goal or objective can be met, the subconscious mind will trigger a pathway to success.

I can recall an incident in my life where I was faced with a huge challenge and somehow I got myself into a fix, but worked my way out with great long term success.

I was Director of Research at the O'Brien Corporation. Every morning I would walk past the Order Department, then on to my office. For some reason one morning I walked past the Vice President's Office instead and he had 6 people standing around and they looked very gloomy. He called me in and told me that PPG was suing O'Brien over the sale and use of Thermosetting Acrylic coatings, since they owned the key patents to that product developed by Dr. Roger Christenson. The group included the Laboratory and Sales Manager and a number of key formulators. A Thermosetting Acrylic was originally patented by Dr. Donald Strain at DuPont, but was unstable and not commercialized. Thermosetting Acrylics revolutionized the coatings industry for automotive, appliance and aircraft finishes.

My response was a shot from the hip or more bluntly a shot from the lip, "**I'll invent something to bypass the PPG patents**".

Everyone burst out into laughter and when the laughter subsided, the VP said, "O.K. Go ahead". I then went on to my office and realized what a blunder I had made. I told my lab assistant what I had done and he informed me that I should get my resume ready since there was no way that I could compete with PPG, who had an army of PhD's available and who did I think I was to challenge such a formidable force.

To make matters worse, the Lab Manager brought me a copy of the Christenson patent and then I realized how deeply I had dug my pit. According to their patent and the many steps involved, O'Brien could never match their effort. This was indeed a sad day for me and I wish I had not taken the path in that day.

When I recovered my senses, I began to examine the chemical structure of thermosetting acrylic developed by PPG. In addition to the many steps required to produce this product, there was a problem of stabilizing the material that vexed Dr. Christenson for a long time.

At that time I was trying to develop a series of water soluble polymers in an effort to produce semi-gloss enamels. In fact, many coatings people were working on the problem. I then realized that by using a certain class of amino alcohols, I would be able to circumvent the PPG patents and achieve my goal. I had my lab assistant start making a series of polymers that indeed circumvented the PPG patents. When the patent was filed, the Patent office decided that we had two inventions, a thermosetting acrylic and an oxazo-line modified thermosetting acrylic resulting in two patents.

Some time later I published a paper on the discovery and compared our method to that of PPG and my good friend Joe Vasta at DuPont phoned me when he read the paper and had a big laugh because of the simplicity of our approach.

Some time after I left O'Brien Corporation, I became a Staff Scientist at Whirlpool. One of my tasks was to interact with the Research Centers of major chemical companies. On a visit to the PPG Research Center, I was taken on a tour of the facility by Dr. Howard Gerhart, the Vice-President and a legendary figure in the Coatings Industry. As we toured the lab, he introduced me to the Director of Research who responded very vocally that he certainly knew me and all the troubles my patents caused him in ther-mosetting acrylics and radiation chemistry.

So we have some lessons here that one should not be afraid of great chal-lenges, even though the task looks hopeless. Secondly the idea of Psycho-Cybernetics can play an enormous role in our travel in life by assuming a positive, can do attitude and rejecting the can't do attitude that leads nowhere. The second lesson is that one must have Faith in oneself and reject to criticism of critics who, in many instances, have a lot less expertise and talent that you may possess. Finally a person must always take advantage of the spiritual Faith taught in the scriptures and the paths that are chosen for us in life. Had I made the wrong turn, I would have never walked past the Vice-President's office and found the opportunity to circumvent the threat to our company.

The Apostle Paul said it well, "I can do all things through Christ who strengthens me" Phil. 4:13

WORRY

When I was a student at San Jose State College, I used to worry a lot! There were some good reasons like a low grade point average that could prevent me from entering teaching, a high work load; 48 hours a week as a movie projectionist and a lack of good sleep that was required of me to keep everything going.

During the beginning of my junior year at San Jose State, I used to spend a lot of time worrying about my grade point average, and my performance in my different classes. In fact, I **probably spent** more time worrying than studying. I used to discuss my problem with friends and apparently bored them with my concern over my academic performance.

One of the classes I was taking was "Conduction of Electricity in Gases", a physics class that was taught by one of the toughest Physics Professors at the college. We had no text for the class, but were required to look up references such as "The 'Particles' of Modern Physics" by J. D. Stranathan and other physics books on Modern Physics.

One afternoon I was in the library looking up these references and for some reason I wandered over into another area of the stacks when I noticed a book, "How to Stop Worrying and Start Living" by Dale Carnegie. I thumbed through the book and decided to check it out even though it had nothing to do with particle physics.

That evening after starting the movie, I began reading the book in earnest.

What a surprise!

I found that I could not put the book down and soon began devouring its contents realizing what a fool I was to spend so much time on worry when positive action on my part was a better choice. This book was a path turner for me and should be required reading in all school curricula. What a difference it would make in students.

Shortly after I completed reading the book I began to follow the sage advice of Dale Carnegie and soon found to my amazement that my grades improved and my attitude toward worry was completely changed.

It is amazing how a book can make such a difference in a life.

If you have not read it, please make sure you do before it is too late. Meanwhile, you can use the Bible until you obtain a copy.

GOOD IDEAS; BAD RESULTS

People are always coming up with ideas, many new, but mostly retreads of old ideas that have not worked in the past. One of the problems with ideas is that the creator becomes so involved in the idea, that many times common sense is over ruled and the consequences of the idea in practice can be disastrous. Congress is well noted for promoting ideas without thoroughly thinking through the consequences of bad legislation.

On example will suffice! Congress was determined to make the rich pay more taxes, so they launched legislation to place an excise tax on luxury boats. The legislation passed and the law enforced. The rich quickly seeing the oncoming taxman responded by purchasing their luxury boats in Spain and other counties, drying up boat manufacturing operations along our gulf coast and elsewhere.

Refrigerator
In the commercial world similar problems occur especially when an eager upwardly mobile executive wants to make a name for himself and rushed a product to market before engineers can fully study the product and determine if there is a potential for failure. This was a bitter lesson for the General Electric Company that rushed to market a new low energy refrigerator using a powdered metal compressor rotor. The idea was good in that expensive manufacturing processes could be eliminated. Whirlpool engineers evaluated such a system and concluded that a powdered metal rotor would fail in the field.

Nevertheless, General Electric pushed the product to market and experienced enormous field failures. My brother in law bought one that went bad. In order to make the repair three technicians arrived at his home early and spent the whole day removing insulation, replacing the compressor and related parts. This good idea cost GE several billion dollars to correct, while the manager who pushed the program, ignoring warning flags and bring the project to completion on time and on budget was promoted to a Vice President post and eventually ironically, was hired by Whirlpool.

Washing Machine

After World War II many of the technical developments of the Manhattan Project found their way into consumer products. One such product application was to the wringer washing machine. This product was responsible for may home accidents as children would have their limbs caught in the rollers or women would have their loose clothing become entangled in the rollers. There were many safety devices designed to disconnect the rollers and these features were important in selling wringer washers to the public.

Whirlpool engineers found that torque sensor technology could be applied to this problem and designed a washing machine that could be reversed by simply pulling back on material being fed into the rollers. This was a major breakthrough and one that would have tremendous marketing appeal.

As with most firms there are many 'dog and pony' shows to review the latest developments for upper management. So, the Laundry Engineering Group put on a show to demonstrate this latest breakthrough, which was very well received by the hierarchy.

Since Sears Roebuck is a major customer of Whirlpool it was important that their buyers and executives see this 'dog and pony' show and a meeting scheduled accordingly. Prior to the meeting, the Director of Engineering queried the engineers to assure that nothing would go wrong. To demonstrate the effect of this new safety device wet Turkish towels were fed into the rollers and upon pulling back, the rollers automatically reversed direction.

The Engineering Director was still skeptical so an engineer put his necktie into the rollers and had him pull back. Upon pulling back, the rollers reversed much to the amazement of the Engineering Director. Everything was now set for the big day. After wining and dining the Sears executives on the previous evening, the Laundry Engineers were eager to demonstrate their masterpiece.

After a discussion of the engineering aspects of the invention, they adjourned to the laboratory to demonstrate the wringer washer. Many Turkish towels were run in and out of the wringer with great success. Finally, a Whirlpool executive took the tie of a Sears executive and fed it into the wringer and guess what happened? The sensor failed and the washer began to strangle the hapless man until the plug was pulled and his tie cut with a scissors.

So much for dog and pony shows.

Aluminum tubing

When I was in high school I worked during the summer at Drew's Cannery as a pie boy then later as an electrician. The cannery began a large expansion that required electrical wiring using steel conduit. Carrying conduit was quite a job especially when we worked high above the floor since the steel tubing was so heavy.

Eventually, aluminum tubing became available and that made the job more pleasant as aluminum is much lighter than steel. Soon many buildings were being wired using aluminum tubing to carry electrical wires in sky scrapers.

Another good idea!

One of the problems with concrete is that it is very porous to water and over time water can migrate into the concrete and reach the aluminum tubing. Since concrete is alkaline water passing through concrete becomes alkaline and that, over time, will dissolve the aluminum much to the dismay of architects who designed the buildings. There was a case of a skyscraper in New York City that lost its ground connection because of the dissolved aluminum tubing! As a result there was a considerable cost to rewire the building to restore grounding capability.

Rebars

One of the very successful products produced by the Dow Chemical Company is SARAN^R a copolymer of vinyl chloride and vinylidene chloride. Various compositions of this material in the form of an emulsion had good adhesion to steel and rendered steel waterproof!

Now here is a great idea for the construction industry. Have you ever seen a construction site where bundles of reinforcing rods lie around ready to be used for reinforced concrete? If you have, you may also noticed rust on these rods indicating the onset of corrosion that can continue after the steel is placed.

So Dow chemists found that they could coat rebars with an emulsion based on this unique copolymer to form a water and moisture barrier insuring less corrosion, that is a massive cost to infra structure all over the world. This opened a great market for this product and illustrates how good ideas can be exploited for good and profit

Later the 'Lightning hit the Outhouse" as reports began to trickle in about some serious corrosion failures similar to the aluminum tubing problem. It seems that vinylidene chloride copolymer tends to degrade over time to hydrochloric acid and the process is catalyzed by iron.

Next case please.

Plumbing Problem

With the discovery of the Ziegler Catalyst for preparing stereospecific polymers , polymer chemists began to explore the polymerization of monomers other than ethylene. One of the monomers tried was 1-butene. This polymer could be prepared in crystalline form and was found to have excellent properties for plumbing applications. As a result many miles of poly-1-butene were extruded and headed for the southwestern part of the United States where builders replaced copper tubing with this polymer. Great idea and another market opened up to plastics.

When first extruded, the polymer is not completely crystallized but over time it gradually increases in crystallization and tends to stress crack.

Imagine all the homes and buildings that had to be retrofitted when this great idea reached the market place.

THE DESK TOP

T. F. Washburn Company was a regional paint manufacturer in Chicago, which formulates and sells Trade Sales paint in the area. In order to increase sales, they try to encourage area distributors to carry their line of paint, which is competitive with other area manufacturers.

One particular distributor came down pretty hard on Washburn countering that they could buy essentially the same paint from Jewel, Standard T or Valspar. The president of the company told the Washburn people to come back only when they had something unique and they would consider selling their paint.

Meanwhile, in Minneapolis General Mills had developed some new chemistry based on fatty amines, that is products derived from the reaction of fatty acids and polyamines. These resins were called "Polyamide resins". When reacted with epoxy resins, they could form a two component coating system with outstanding properties

Polyamides could also be used to make alkyd resins. An unusual property of polyamide alkyds was that they could be formulated into a thixotropic paint. The paint simply did not flow and the can could be turned upside down and no paint would pour out. However, when a brush is inserted into the paint, the paint could be applied to a surface without dripping or spattering.

In order to develop a market for this, General Mills made an agreement with Washburn to formulate a line of alkyd paints which could be advertised as non-drip, non-spattering paint.

THIS WOULD BE A MARKET SENSATION!!!

Armed with this potent new marketing tool, the Washburn people sought and obtained an appointment with the president of the distribution company for 11:00 a.m. on next Tuesday.

THEY HAD A REAL SURPRISE FOR HIM!!

On the appointed day, the Washburn people entered the president's office with a quart of their new thixotropic paint. But, instead of demonstrating the paint, the company president wanted to show off his new desk. He had just spent a fortune on an imported hand carved desk and everyone oohed and aahed over this beautiful desk until noon.

It was now lunchtime so the company president suggested they delay the demo until after lunch. He suggested he drive his big Cadillac so they all piled in and put the paint can on the rear shelf to be warmed in the sun during a lengthy lunch.

After lunch they returned to the president's office and made their pitch. Here was something a paint that won't drip or spatter. The Washburn salesman proceeded to open the can of paint and tipped it upside down. The paint came rushing out of the can all over the imported desk...ruining the top of the desk.

Washburn did not make a sale, but they did get the opportunity to pay for refinishing the ruined desk.

Polyamides anyone?

THE TOILET SEAT AFFAIR

In the early sixties, epoxy resins were making a big splash in the coatings industry. They were being heralded for pipe coatings because of their superior corrosion and abrasion resistance.

Another big event that revolutionized the coatings industry was the introduction into trade sales applications of a two component epoxy resin system which had remarkable properties. This system consisted of a component of EPON 1001® and a Versamid® polyamide resin sold by General Mills. This remarkable coating had a high gloss, excellent adhesion, chemical, and water resistance . Coatings made from this system made excellent swimming pool liners and many pool owners had the coating applied to their pools. Other applications followed.

The O'Brien Corporation marketed a version of this and called it MiraPlate® and its marketing director began to find as many applications as possible. One application evolved in which it was determined that MiraPlate® was great for refurbishing toilet seats. The procedure was to mix component A the epoxy fraction, with component B the polyamide fraction, allow it to sit for one hour then apply. It took about 12 hours for cure.

A certain homeowner bought some MiraPlate® and applied it to the seat in his home. That evening he and his wife attended a function and hired a baby sitter, but forgot to inform the baby sitter of the new breakthrough in the bathroom. Sometime during the evening, after putting the children to bed the baby sitter required a visit to the MiraPlate® coated toilet seat. But, as the babysitter tried to stand up, the excellent adhesive properties of the coating prevented her from rising...she was fixed to the seat.

She was finally able to rouse one of the children, who called the fire department. When they arrived, they too were not up to the adhesive properties of the epoxy coating. They in turn called a physician. When the physician arrived and saw the situation, he burst out laughing so hard he fell into the tub and broke his jaw. The firemen then tried solvents to no avail.

Finally, two burly firemen grabbed the poor girl by the arms and jerked her off the seat along with a layer of epoxy paint.

*****

Part IV

REFLECTIONS

FINDING A TREASURE

A family friend wrote me the other day and asked me, "How did you find Carol and when did you fall in love with her?" I said, "Delaney, it was by osmosis"

In truth the way I found this treasure of a wife and mother and outstanding teacher is by the hand of our God. In the scriptures we are taught:

"I will instruct you and teach you in the way that you will go; I will guide you with my eye" Ps 32:8

Fifty nine years ago I had just started teaching at San Jose State College. Carol who was unhappy at home was looking for a good husband. So each morning she would take a bus from Palo Alto to San Jose, walk over to St. Joseph's Church and pray: "DEAR ST. JOE, SEND ME A BEAU, AND NEVER LET HIM GO"

The first day of class I walked in looking like a used car salesman and wrote my name on the board. Carol said to herself...THAT'S HIM!

Little did I know that I had been targeted. Soon Miss Mott would show up at my office to ask for help on problems (she and our later Bridesmaid Anna Rimkus) were the smartest in the class. So I would go over problems, and she would just hang around.

I lived with my mother and sister and my mother would make me sandwiches like peanut butter and jelly. So one day my mother told me she was going to make me a ham sandwich. This was great and I looked forward to a real lunch. As a matter of fact, I spent more time thinking of the sandwich than of chemistry.

After class, I hurried to my office and my ham sandwich when, you guessed it, Carol Mott shows up with more chemistry questions. I worked a few problems and waited for her to leave but she stayed on so finally asked her if she would like to have half of my sandwich. "Sure" she said, then proceeded to devour all of my sandwich.

If we ponder this scripture we see key words, instruct, teach and guide.

Carol has been all of that in her full life. At age 15 she began to teach in her neighborhood for 25 cents a lesson, then went on to be one of the best teachers in the area teaching organ, piano and violin from ages 5 to 70. She has spread her love and kindness to many families by her example where teaching music was more than notes. Her students came away with more treasure than they sought. She was able to recognize and encourage talent in her many students. She has been an inspirational guide for many families in this area.

She taught at IUSB though she did not have a degree in music, but after I retired she obtained a degree in Piano Performance with High Distinction.

Twelve years ago she was struck down with cancer and told that she would never walk again. Her faith in Jesus and the love of Mary Pat Russ, a therapist, she walked again. She would pray each night that if she could only touch the hem of His garment, she would walk again. And walk she did.

To thank God for His mercy she dedicated her garden to God and her beautiful garden is called God's Garden.

She was known by many in this area as the "Lady with the Garden". One day a woman stopped by and told her that her mother was dying of cancer and whenever they took her for a ride she would always ask to drive by the Lady with the Garden.

So, farewell Carol and I know that the gardens of Heaven will now be weed free with you there.

I love you Carol

CAROL IS BACK

Carol died on October 5, 2011 on the Feast Day of St. Faustina. As I sat beside her on that day, I had no idea that she was going away, but she did. We sat with her for two hours and surely expected her to wake up again, but she was gone!

There are many tales about dying and what happens after one dies. One of particular interest is that the soul of the departed lingers for three days, then departs the earth. During that time the spirit can and sometimes leave a message to the bereaved. A good friend of ours told us a tale of a departed relative. She and her husband went to the home of the departed and the wife went to the cellar, one of those with slanted doors. While she was down there the cellar door closed on her. She shouted for her husband who came and opened the door. After he convinced her that he was not the one who closed the door, they went into the house, whereupon the weights of the clock were lifted up by invisible hands in front of their very eyes and much to their shock.

The idea of a soul remaining on earth for three days makes sense, since putrefaction does not set in until the fourth day. This was clearly shown in the case of Lazarus. When Jesus learned of his illness, he tarried for two more days, so that when Jesus reached Bethany Lazarus was dead for four days. Jesus then raised Lazarus and that was His death sentence since the Pharisees were outraged at Jesus because He represented a threat to their power.

During the days after Carol's departure we saw signs that she was still with us. To wit, the day after her death a large buck deer walked out of the woods and to our apple orchard. He was not afraid, but stood around so we could take pictures of him, then he slowly walked back to the woods.

This evening while our family gathered around the patio near sunset, Beamer felt someone touch his shoulder and direct him to look at the wine patio. Much to our surprise we saw a brilliant sun dog that radiated rainbow color down on us and focused on the wine patio where Carol and I used to spend our evening hours after taking care of God's Garden. We then realized that Carol was watching us and sent us a last farewell and look at her beautiful garden that she dedicated to God for his mercy in curing her of her paralysis and gave us twelve more years of bliss, before He called her home to care for His heavenly paradise.

God Bless you Dear Carol and Thank You for letting us know you were here on this beautiful Friday evening.

WHERE IS MY PET?

During Carol's waning battle with cancer, she always carried her pet. Her pet is a small cloth bag with oriental designs and made for her by Connie Yeh, a relative of Daisy and David Yeh. Connie lives in Taiwan and on one of her visits here she gave the pet to Carol. Carol treasured the pet and carried it everywhere she went.

Her pet contained some real treasure and she protected it with her life. If you looked into her *pet* you would find a comb or two, several tubes of CARMEX lip balm and some tweezers. There were many nights after we had finished our evening prayers, that she would panic because she could not find her *pet!* Then she would remember that she left it in the studio and so I would get out of bed and go downstairs to retrieve it, much to her comfort. Whenever she went for some hospital test she would make sure she had her beloved *pet.*

The night before she died, she woke me several times during the night because she could not find her *pet* under her covers. So her *pet* was everywhere she was up to her last church visit in her casket, along with some weeds, since she loved to weed her garden.

The Sunday after her death her beloved Sweetie died. She was our rescued Greyhound and she loved Carol. When our first Greyhound, Wake, died we sought another dog and Nancy and Jim Moffett recommended Sweetie a three year old red and white grey full of puppy behavior.

After considering Carol's health condition, Jim suggested we not take her but choose another dog and assured us that Sweetie would be adopted. So we came home with Benne and Miki. As we brought them into the family room Carol burst into tears since we had left Sweetie behind. Several weeks later I was looking at the Great Lakes Greyhound website and noticed that Benne and Miki were listed as adopted, and lo and behold Sweetie was still up for adoption. Carol raced for the phone and told Jim and Nancy that we would come and get her. Whoever adopted her said that she had fleas and gave her up. We rushed to Merrillville and brought her home. Sweetie was a real puppy. She would take her toys that Aunt Irene sent her and run around the family room squeaking them and throwing them into the air. Benne and Miki were more reserved. These dogs were really loved and we enjoyed sharing their love with friends. On Dog Blessing Day we took them to St. Piux X where Msgr. Schooler would bless the animals. He liked these pups since, whenever I went to confession, he would always remind me to take care of the Greyhounds.

Meanwhile, back in Heaven Carol asked for her pet. Scriptures tell us that in order to stay in Heaven one must have a pet; cat or dog (preferably a Greyhound) to assure their place in Heaven*. So Carol sent for her pet, but because of a clerical error, they came for Sweetie instead of the *pet*.

At any rate, Carol and Sweetie had definitely made a hit in Heaven, and I plan to keep the *Pet* for her until Carol decides to come and take me to join her and Sweetie.

IF THIS IS NOT IN THE BIBLE, IT SHOULD BE!!

CONFIRMATION

One of the very important Sacraments of the Catholic Church is that of Confirmation. At this event the candidate receives the Gift of the Holy Spirit. A lot of preparation is required for this great event, but I wonder how many people, mostly children, really understand the importance of the moment and the effect on their whole lives?

I remember receiving this sacrament in the fourth grade and really did not think too much about it except that the nuns were so strict that we stay in line, wore ties and above all wear shoes. (In Honolulu we never wore shoes to school; we were barefooted). I also wonder if being confirmed at an early age makes much sense regarding the importance of this sacred event!

During the act of confirmation, we receive in fact the MIND OF GOD! There is a spiritual transformation wherein if prepared, one can soar to great heights or just go on being the same person as before. We therefore should reflect on this important event by looking at the impact the Holy Spirit has had on humans.

Jesus was a carpenter and a rabbi until He visited his cousin John the Baptist where Jesus was baptized with the Water of Salvation. At that event Jesus also received the Power of the Holy Spirit and at that point immediately went to the desert to complete His spiritual journey. Jesus now had the Kingdom, Power and Majesty of God.

If we consider the apostles we find that, with some exception, they were unlearned men and in no way could compare to the learned Pharisees who had so much power over them due to their knowledge of scripture and the Law. This is why the apostles were always confounded at the works of Jesus. But, when that fateful Pentecost occurred, the apostles became spiritual giants, since they now possessed the Mind of God and a direct contact with the Holy Spirit. They confounded the Pharisees with their knowledge because they now lived in power of the Holy Spirit. Read the Acts of the Apostles to confirm this belief.

We too can have that power if we learn to understand the meaning of Confirmation and realize that from that day forward, the Holy Spirit dwells in you. You can reject this gift at your own peril or grow to become like Him. Always keep in mind this verse:

"**Let the words of my mouth and the meditation of my heart be acceptable in your sight O Lord my strength and my Redeemer**" Ps. 19:14

DONNA'S HERE

One of the great traits of my dear wife Carol was that she always had to have some project going, whether it was a garden bed, or remodeling the house. I had a nice study where our Cat Library is now and she decided to make me a bigger office. That involved major changes that gave us a cathedral ceiling in the family room and much more space. Then she decided to redo the whole kitchen and we hired Weinberg Custom Homes to completely strip out and rebuild the old kitchen since Tom had done a lot of excellent work on our home.

One of Carol's music students gave her a bracelet that could be modified with different links portraying many different icons. Whenever I needed a surprise or gift for Carol, I would go to Inspire Me to buy links for her bracelet. For Valentine's Day I offered to buy her three links so we went to the store. The lady who waited on us seemed to us to be someone special. As she was assembling the new links she asked Carol how she got started on this and Carol said that one of her piano students gave her the first bracelet. This lady said that she had a son who would like to study piano and would like to call Carol to arrange for her son to begin lessons. Usually, conversations like this have little or no follow through.

Much to our surprise and good fortune Donna Kash did call indeed and Carol took Spenser as a student. Donna turned out to be more than a student's mother! She invited Carol and I to a family dinner and we met other members of her family and have been good friends ever since.

Shortly after meeting Donna, I came down with anemia and congestive heart failure. I can never forget Donna and Spenser coming to visit me at the hospital and for their sincere concern for Carol and I. Donna and Spenser also brought a nice box of chocolates that made me a hit with the nurses.

After I recovered I would have problems with depression and Carol diagnosed the illness as being bored; though I tried to argue my way out of it, she was right. One afternoon, as Carol was teaching, Tom and I watched the 3:30 episode of the Lone Ranger. Then I told Tom Weinberg that I had to go to bed since I was so sick. So I got into bed feeling sorry for myself, when Tom shouted up the stairs:

"DONNA IS HERE"

I leaped out of bed like a 'mormon on a mission', dressed and flew downstairs. Carol had finished teaching and joined Donna and me in the family room. For some reason Tom seemed to lose interest in the kitchen project as long as Donna was here. My illness vanished as soon as Donna arrived!

Carol and I have loved Donna ever since and consider her an Angel Sent!

EASTER SEASON

When Grandpa Bigdog lived in Honolulu there were a lot of interesting activities that occurred. For example New Years Eve was a big night and the whole city sounded like a war zone from all the firecrackers that people set off.

Another interesting event was the Holy Ghost festival. This was sponsored by the Holy Ghost Society, a group of Portagees who held an annual festival on the grounds of the Holy Ghost Chapel that was situated on top of Holy Ghost Hill. This consisted of a parade of the Holy Ghost Shrine down Pouwaina Drive and we kids would be pressed into service to march in the parade so we could get punch and cookies after the parade. The parade also featured the Kalihi Orphanage Band that marched and later played music as the Portagee ladies played bingo.

GBD lived on the slopes of Punchbowl, an extinct volcanic tuff crater, and we spent a lot of time on that mountain. We moved from Auwaiolimu Street to 1822-A Boyd lane that is just off Lusitana Street. Uncle Paul, Uncle Wally and GBD used to walk up to Punchbowl by going past Eddie Medeiros house, up Holy Ghost Hill (Concordia Street) then up Puowaina Drive that wound around near the base of the crater past Papakoulea, a Hawaiian settlement, then into the crater itself.

The road into the crater was lined with pinini plants (cactus) and koa bushes as well as a lot of grass. The army used the crater for target practice and soldiers from the various forts would come there for target shooting. On the makai side of the crater there was a large masonry platform where we used to sit to look over the island. (This was also the place where GBD and Uncle Paul got the wits scared out of us when one of our friends told us about Frankenstein and the Werewolf).

As Easter approached there were some interesting events that occurred in Honolulu. We attended Blessed Sacrament Church on Pauoa Street and we had Stations of the Cross and other services during Easter week.

One of the most memorable events for GBD and Uncle Paul was when they placed a huge cross on the masonry platform atop Punchbowl. We would walk up to Punchbowl to observe the setting in place of this cross. Then at night the big excitement was to go down to the corner where Pouwaina Drive and Emma Street merged. At that point across from Kunimoto's Grocery Store was a small park. The U. S. Army would bring two large searchlights and a generator there and set up shop for Easter week. The reason they needed two was because they burned carbon rods to produce an intense light and the rods burnt out after awhile, so they needed a second light while the other cooled and the carbon rods were replaced.

At night they would fire up those large arc lights and shine their beam onto the cross that was sitting on top of Punchbowl projecting the outline of the cross into the sky for everyone to see from miles around. It is one of the most memorable sights GBD could ever remember and a fitting tribute to our Lord who made our salvation possible by dying on the Cross.

GUIDE

"I will instruct thee and teach thee in the way which thou shall go; I will guide thee with mine eye" Ps. 32:8

When I was attending Campbell Union High School in California I was a member of the *EL LOBO HI-Y.* This was a boy's club that included Ray Flagg, Harold Ely, Kent Clark and Larry Lewis. Our faculty advisor was Mr. C. P. Klassen.

At the last meeting of the club year, Mr. Klassen announced that he had gifts for the graduating seniors. I eagerly opened my gift and found out it was not a gift, it was a New Testament. I had expected a real gift like a pen or a pocket knife. He then asked if he could autograph our copies which he did. I then took the gift and threw it into a dresser drawer and forgot about it.

After graduating, I became a movie projectionist at the Campbell Theater and one day I took my gift to work to help pass the time away. I began reading all the begats in Matthew until I reached the Sermon on the Mount and then I realized what a treasure this man had given me. I looked back at the inscription and it read:

> **To:** **Tom Miranda**
> **From: C. P. Klassen**
> **Ps. 32: 8**

I still recite this verse each day and reflect upon the power in that simple line. It deals with teaching, guidance and showing us the way as directed by God. Many times we can reflect on our accomplishments without recognizing the input from our Savior in directing our path and the strange ways God knows our plans far into the future.

After graduation from Notre Dame I served as Director of Research for the O'Brien Corporation. After eight years I began to realize that I was in a no growth situation and the culture was not a good match for my technical expertise. In fact my future there was bleak.

One day the Industrial Coatings Manager came in and told us that we were in trouble! Whirlpool was sending one of their Research Engineers, Euclid Faneuf, to evaluate our technical expertise and he felt that we had no one to talk to him. I volunteered to take up the challenge.

Mr. Faneuf was a real tough customer and did a lot of probing and challenging of our technology base, He had been assigned a task to evaluate the technology of Whirlpool's paint suppliers and their research outlook.

I took Mr. Faneuf through our labs and manufacturing operations and then sat down to talk technology with him. I gave him copies of my publications and patents in Radiation Chemistry, Water Soluble Polymers and Thermosetting Acrylics.

A year after his visit I decided it was time to leave O'Brien and I started looking for work. Carol and I had just started remodeling our home and there were no real jobs in town. I had several offers in Chicago but did not want to leave here. I finally accepted a position with Uni Royal in Mishawaka beginning in late March. Uni Royal was planning to move its operations to Connecticut after a year, but it was a job in town. So I resigned myself to that situation.

I was at the bottom of the barrel in attitude and internal turmoil at work. I did a final interview at Wheelabrator and was told that I was over qualified for the job. I returned to my office and was ready to leave when the phone rang. It was Dr. Day at Whirlpool and he asked me if I could send them my resume'. This I did and the next day I was called for an interview which turned out to be like a 'done deal' and I was hired. After a year there I was promoted to Staff Scientist and retired as Head of the Material Science Department. Euclid Faneuf was now in my department and ready to retire so we threw a big party for him.

As he was cleaning out his desk, he gave me a copy of his Research Report that he had done twenty years earlier. I read the report and was stunned by the last line of his conclusions that read:

"If Whirlpool ever needs a coatings expert, I would strongly recommend that we hire Dr. Miranda"

God works in strange ways and this is not only a good example of His ways it is also a powerful lesson as written in Ps. 32:8.

So indeed, He was instructing me, guiding me and teaching me in the way I would go.

HUMBLE

"Humble yourself therefore under the mighty hand of God that He may exalt you in due time"
1 Pet. 5:5

The bible is a treasure of valuable information that in many instances can be applied to the individual in any type of circumstance. In fact at the beginning of many bibles [Gideon] there are keywords that can lead a person in distress to verses that have a soothing effect or give answer to a problem that maybe causing someone to experience a stressful situation. This is why many people use the bible daily to scan for support in carrying out our daily journey through life.

When I was at Whirlpool, the first thing I did on reaching my office was to look up a bible verse and write it at the top of my daily work list. Then I wrote the particular reference i.e. Prov. 3:5 on a sheet of paper and sent it to friends around the corporation using the interoffice mail. One day I received a reply from a friend at our Danville, Kentucky division who told me that the verse I had sent came at the right time and helped him through the day.

St. Peter reminds us that in our trials we must humble ourselves and eventually things will work out, many times much better than we could ever dream, because "He cares for you".

There is a principle referred to as the 10,000 hour rule. The author suggests that to be ultimately successful you must spend ten thousand hours toward achieving that goal. Two examples will suffice to illustrate this rule. In the first Bill Gates spent that much time pursuing his dream of learning the technology of computers that allowed him to start a revolution in computers. Captain Sullenberger who successfully landed his plane in the Hudson River, had over 10,000 hours of flying that prepared him for his heroic effort when his plane was downed by a bird impact collision.

Sometimes we labor for a long time and never seem to reach a definitive goal or a successful outcome. I remember when I was in college I worked 6 to 7 days a week to support my mother and sister who was also attending college. After completing my Masters Degree in Physical Science I was still working as a projectionist at the Sunnyvale Theater. It seems that I would never get anywhere. But one day all that changed! I received a call from Dr. Naylor the Head of the Chemistry Department at San Jose State and he offered me a job teaching chemistry. Then things changed big time! I met Carol and my whole life changed. It seems that God had to humble me for the life He had prepared for us.

My mother had a humble life when my father died at age 37 leaving her with 5 young children and on welfare. She taught us to pray and made sure we attended church. We would gather around our dinner table every evening to pray the rosary and she made sure we behaved ourselves. After Carol and I were married her humility came to a bright end. She married her childhood friend who had a 300 acre ranch in Hawaii and he gave her all the things she was denied during our growing up. God never forgot her humility and exalted her in the end with a rewarding life that she had never had.

You too, are never forgotten and God can exalt you in due time.

ONE THIRTY NINE

My high school algebra teacher, C. P. Klassen was a great Christian and an excellent teacher. He once gave me a New Testament and pointed out Psalm 32:8 that is must reading for anyone. Another quote he led me to was Ps 19:14. These treasures have been with me since I left high school and I recite them every day. Bible quotes are useful road signs to our passage through life.

In 2005 a colleague of mine, Dr. Eugene C. Ashby published "*Understanding the Creation/Evolution Controversy*. This book presents a scientific evaluation consistent with Modern Science and the Bible. [Dr. Ashby is Regents Professor and Distinguished Professor of Chemistry and Biochemistry, Emeritus at the Georgia Institute of Technology.] He and I were graduate students at Notre Dame in the fifties.

After publishing his book, Gene had worked to promote the book and to attract the attention of the news and religious community to the content of his book and he was willing to engage in debate regarding his conclusions on this important subject. He was invited to participate in a debate at San Diego Community College where the liberal faculty was ready to challenge his views. In fact, the projection equipment had been stolen from the auditorium just prior to his presentation. Gene, with the power of the Holy Spirit addressed the students and told them he was speaking to them, since they made up over 85% of the audience. The question and answer period lasted over 30 minutes until it ran into his time to give a lecture at the Chemistry Department. After his chemistry lecture the questions continued about his views on evolution and this issue was later posted on the internet.

After that Gene sent letters to friends telling us of his success and concluded his letter with a quote from Psalm 139: 1-16. I read the psalm and for some reason it did not strike a chord in me. Last year Carol and I began attending Holy Hour on Friday and during that time I read my Gideon New Testament. It was during one of these sessions I really read the Psalm and became involved in its true meaning. [I believe many people read words and not the meaning of the treasure hidden in the bible.] This was true for me also since I now read that every week, but continually mull over the true meaning of that Psalm every day.

What is immediately obvious is that we cannot escape from God. This is an awesome truth with many implications for Christians. An awesome thought is that the light and the darkness are the same to God and since He is with us always, how should we behave? Furthermore, how about our daily thoughts and deeds? If we really take the meaning of this psalm to heart, it would be a perfect guide for our daily travel to eternity and how we carry out our relationships with God and our fellow men. The very fact that God is interested in us even before our conception is awesome.

A daily reflection on the words in Psalm 139 should lead the Christian to a better life on earth.

THE STATUE

Carol was a master gardener and she called her garden God's Garden because He helped her to walk after being paralyzed by a thyroid tumor on her spine. As we were on our journey through life, she was always thinking of new things to do or new gardens to plant. When grass did not grow well under some trees she would build a garden over the area. The idea of her building a new garden came with some unexpected benefits. That is, it meant that we had to scour the local area looking for rocks to outline the bed then the live in half-wit (that's me) would be invited to haul dirt to fill in the area where the garden would be. Then she would name the garden. For example the large garden behind the studio would be called The Island Bed and the garden by the pool became the Angel Garden. She lived for her music and gardens and I could never let her down.

During our growth period Carol kept inviting me to get a hobby. It seems that I spent too much time on Polymer Chemistry and never backed off to more relaxing endeavors. After much prodding I finally settled on beekeeping. So each evening when I returned from work, the first thing I would do was to walk down to the beehives and see how my pets were doing then go in to greet Carol and the children. After changing in to work clothes, I would walk around the yard and was usually shocked to see a large piece of lawn laid out with water hose. This meant that another garden was planned. This one was the Day Lily bed behind the studio.

She had laid out a large circle and that meant that all the sod would have to be removed. This task involved a lot of African Automation; lots of shovel work. I would always swear that if she ever started another garden I would join a church, since I am convinced that hell is made up of sod removal crews. After removing the sod I was invited to till the ground several times, until she was ready to plant her lilies. Then she asked Greg Ballew to edge the bed with plastic edging to complete the task.

There is an antique store on the corner of Gumwood and SR 23 that had a number of beautiful statues about five feet high and Carol expressed some interest in buying one. Since I liked to surprise her with under pillow gifts, I turned to lying* to accomplish the task. I told her that I had looked at the statues and they were cracked and of poor quality. So one day I visited the place and made a deal with the owner to deliver the statue while we were gone to Bloomington. Our daughter Irene came to stay with the house in our absence and supervised the placement of the statue in the center of her lily garden.

All the way to and from Bloomington she talked about the statue and was determined to get one the day we returned. So we arrived home and had dinner, Carol reminding me about buying the statue until she looked out the window and saw the beautiful lady statue that stands there reminding us of the Beautiful Lady with the Garden, Carol.

---

*I really did not lie; I was only careless with the Truth!

THE PERFECT PARTNER

"Let the words of my mouth and the meditation of my heart, be acceptable in your sight, O Lord, my strength and my Redeemer" Ps 19:14

I first learned this verse from my high school algebra teacher, C. P. Klassen. He was an excellent teacher and cared a lot for his students and for the little town of Campbell. I have remembered this verse since then and say it every morning the moment I awake. There is a lot of power in this verse since it makes the individual responsible for establishing a clear contact path to our Lord Jesus Christ, especially when we need help.

In the business world there are many problems that occur that may at times exceed the area of expertise of the in house people. As a result many firms engage consultants to overcome roadblocks that may occur on the way to completing a task. The consultant may be used for a short time or over a long period of time, but knowing that consultation is available is a comfort to those who use good consultants.

I recall an experience I had with Boeing Aircraft Company in Seattle. One day I received a phone call asking me for some help in the area of Chemical Milling. After spending some time on the phone, I was able to direct them to a solution to their problem. That service was convenient and fast and demonstrated what a consultant can do for a client.

In our daily life we too have a need for a consultant who is ready and eager to assist us in solving both small and large problems. This consultant is available always and responds to our requests in ways that to us have long-term benefits.

That consultant is the Lord Jesus Christ. If you consider Jesus as a partner in your every day activities then you will be amazed how He can make your life an exciting and pleasurable experience. The cost of His services is spelled out in the above verse. In order to have access to the Lord we must maintain a state of mind and heart that will allow instant communication between us and Him. If your heart is not right, it is more difficult to obtain His attention as noted in the verse cited.

Give Him a try! The next time you have a problem go to Jesus first and lay out your problem to Him, being sure that your heart is in tune with His and see what happens. From small requests to major needs He will hear your prayer and answer accordingly, because He cares for you. And don't forget to thank Him for watching over you each day of your life.

Remember to set your heart straight and nothing will be impossible for you.

FAMOUS UNKNOWNS

An interesting characteristic in people is their need for attention. Dale Carnegie noted this in his famous book "How to Win Friends and Influence People". One of his comments was that people like to hear their name. One can test this idea easily. For example, when I am in the checkout lane at the store, I read the clerks name and recite it as I leave. The normal reaction is that in most cases people are pleased to hear their name.

Many people seek popularity by having their names spread around in the media and print. Movie stars, politicians and celebrities seek after this type of exposure. That leads to a road to fame (or infamy) and a path to power. Some people in Hollywood rent limousines to ride around and stoke their need for fame and celebrity.

Some famous people include Alexander the Great, Attila the Hun and their ilk who became famous by their military deeds and brutality from which they received their power. It is interesting to watch, in our own time, people who seek to be famous. Some members of congress are a real danger to others if someone stands between them and a TV camera.

But what about people who are not striving to become famous and through no fault of theirs become eternal legends? There are a number of interesting examples in the scriptures.

Consider Simon of Cyrene. He was coming into town for the Passover celebration and not seeking fame, yet he became eternally famous by carrying the Cross of Jesus. Another example is the woman who poured spikenard over Jesus as an act of Love. This was an expensive spice, yet she emptied all of it on Jesus. For her act of Love, Jesus prophesied that her act will be remembered through the ages.

Veronica was probably just another Palestinian woman, but her courageous effort to risk death and go to Jesus to wipe His face earned her place forever in the history of the world and she was rewarded with an image of His face on her towel. Other unknowns that became famous include the Good Samaritan, the Woman at the Well and the Samaritan leper, who of the ten cured, returned to give glory to God and entered history forever. Finally, the Centurion who asked Jesus for healing of his servant is remarkable. This man was a pagan and not interested in other religious beliefs, yet he recognized the authority that Jesus represented and has been rewarded ever since in every Sunday mass at communion.

The bible reminds us that God works in strange ways. The above gives credence to this reminder and we need to put our Trust in the Lord Jesus in our everyday activities, because we never know when His guiding hand will intervene in your life.

The apostle Peter was on target when he wrote: "**Humble yourselves therefore under the mighty hand of God, that He may exalt you in due time**" 1Pet 5:6

*****

SUMMARY

This book contains a compilation of stories that provide first a warning of where we are headed as a nation then traces the authors life from growing up in poverty and climbing out of the well of dependency to achieving a place in the American Dream that includes hard work and commitment to principles of responsible citizenship. In growing up there are many events that remain in the mind forever. Growing up experiences can be depressing, a learning experience or a guide to future behavior. It is remarkable that some seemingly unimportant event can and does play a role in later life that can be rewarding of disappointing. In this book the author mentions taking the wrong turn to his office that had a significant effect in later technical applications. Finally, the loss of a loved one reminds one of the importance of interpersonal relationships such as taking for granted a loved ones daily contribution to ones daily life.

Acknowledgement

The author is especially grateful to the support and love of our dear friends who have stood by Carol and me during our journey through life. Special thanks to Donna Kash, Irene and George Pospolita, Christine Forry, Dr. Wendell Garcia, Mary Pat Russ and Thomas K. Weinberg. Sincere appreciation and love to Carol's many students and their families; **ALL OF HER TREASURES.**

ABOUT THE AUTHOR

Thomas J. Miranda, is a native of Hawaii and has been active in the field of Polymer Chemistry and Coatings Technology for over forty years. His achievements as scientist, inventor, author and lecturer are well documented in polymer synthesis, heterogeneous catalysis, polymer stabilization, water soluble polymers, emulsion technology and radiation chemistry.

The author was born in Ewa, Oahu on a sugar plantation and grew up in Honolulu living there until a year after the Pearl Harbor bombing that he witnessed. He moved to California, graduated from San Jose State College with an AB and MA in Physical Sciences and taught there for one year. He served in the Army Chemical Corps, then received a PhD in Organic Chemistry from Notre Dame University where he was the W.R. Grace Research Fellow and an MSBA from Indiana University where he taught as an Adjunct Assistant Professor of Chemistry over a twenty year period.

His business experiences include Director of Research for the O'Brien Corporation, Staff Scientist at Whirlpool Corporation. He served as President of the Paint Research Institute, Technical Editor for the Federation of Societies for Coatings Technology's *Journal of Coatings Technology* for twenty years and Editor of the Monograph Series on Coatings Technology. He served as an Industrial Consultant in the Materials Science area.

He received a number of local and National Awards for Outstanding Scientific Accomplishment and the Distinguished Business Alumnus Award from the Business School of Indiana University South Bend.

He is the author of *Growing up in Hawaii* and has published over 50 papers, book chapters and the author of 13 United States Patents

CPSIA information can be obtained
at www.ICGtesting.com
Printed in the USA
FFOW05n0024030114